American Addresses

With A Lecture On The Study Of Biology

by

Thomas Henry Huxley

AMERICAN ADDRESSES
WITH A LECTURE ON THE STUDY OF BIOLOGY
by Thomas Henry Huxley

ISBN: 978-93-59321-16-5

Published by

DOUBLE 9 BOOKS

2/13-B, Ansari Road, Daryaganj
New Delhi – 110002
info@double9books.com
www.double9books.com
Tel. 011-40042856

ABOUT THE AUTHOR

Thomas Henry Huxley (May 4, 1825 – June 29, 1895) was an English scientist and anthropologist who specialized in comparative anatomy. He became known as "Darwin's Bulldog" because of his support for Charles Darwin's theory of evolution. Although some historians believe that the surviving tale of Huxley's famous 1860 Oxford evolution discussion with Samuel Wilberforce is a later invention, it was a pivotal occasion in the wider acceptance of evolution and in his own career. Huxley had planned to leave Oxford the day before, but after meeting Robert Chambers, the author of Vestiges, he changed his mind and chose to participate in the debate. Richard Owen, with whom Huxley also discussed whether humans were closely connected to apes, coached Wilberforce. Huxley was slow to adopt certain of Darwin's concepts, including as gradualism, and was undecided about natural selection, but he was a staunch supporter of Darwin in public. He was instrumental in promoting scientific education in Britain, and he fought against more radical religious traditions. Huxley invented the term "agnosticism" in 1869 and expanded on it in 1889 to define the nature of claims in terms of what is and is not knowable.

CONTENTS

NEW YORK

LECTURES ON EVOLUTION

LECTURE I
THE THREE HYPOTHESES RESPECTING THE HISTORY OF NATURE

We live in and form part of a system of things of immense diversity and perplexity, which we call Nature; and it is a matter of the deepest interest to all of us that we should form just conceptions of the constitution of that system and of its past history. With relation to this universe, man is, in extent, little more than a mathematical point; in duration but a fleeting shadow; he is a mere reed shaken in the winds of force. But, as Pascal long ago remarked, although a mere reed, he is a thinking reed; and in virtue of that wonderful capacity of thought, he has the power of framing for himself a symbolic conception of the universe, which, although doubtless highly imperfect and inadequate as a picture of the great whole, is yet sufficient to serve him as a chart for the guidance of his practical affairs. It has taken long ages of toilsome and often fruitless labour to enable man to look steadily at the shifting scenes of the phantasmagoria of Nature, to notice what is fixed among her fluctuations, and what is regular among her apparent irregularities; and it is only comparatively lately, within the last few centuries, that the conception of a universal order and of a definite course of things, which we term the course of Nature, has emerged.

But, once originated, the conception of the constancy of the order of Nature has become the dominant idea of modern thought. To any person who is familiar with the facts upon which that conception is based, and is competent to estimate their significance, it has ceased to be conceivable that chance should have any place in the universe, or that events should depend upon any but the natural sequence of cause and effect. We have come to look upon the present as the child of the past and as the parent of the future; and, as we have excluded chance from a place in the universe, so we ignore, even as a possibility, the notion of any interference with the order of Nature. Whatever may be men's speculative doctrines, it is quite certain, that every intelligent person guides his life and risks his fortune upon the belief that the order of Nature is constant, and that the chain of natural causation is never broken.

In fact, no belief which we entertain has so complete a logical basis as that to which I have just referred. It tacitly underlies every process of reasoning; it is the foundation of every act of the will. It is based upon the broadest induction, and it is verified by the most constant, regular, and universal of deductive processes. But we must recollect that any human belief, however broad its basis, however defensible it may seem, is, after all, only a probable belief, and that our widest and safest generalizations are simply statements of the highest degree of probability. Though we are quite clear about the constancy of the order of Nature, at the present time, and in the present state of things, it by no means necessarily follows that we are justified in expanding this generalisation into the infinite past, and in denying, absolutely, that there may have been a time when Nature did not follow a fixed order, when the relations of cause and effect were not definite, and when extra-natural agencies interfered with the general course of Nature. Cautious men will allow that a universe so different from that which we know may have existed; just as a very candid thinker may admit that a world in which two and two do not make four, and in which two straight lines do inclose a space, may exist. But the same caution which forces the admission of such possibilities demands a great deal of evidence before it recognises them to be anything more substantial. And when it is asserted that, so many thousand years ago, events occurred in a manner utterly foreign to and inconsistent with the existing laws of Nature, men, who without being particularly cautious, are simply honest thinkers, unwilling to deceive themselves or delude others, ask for trustworthy evidence of the fact.

Did things so happen or did they not? This is a historical question, and one the answer to which must be sought in the same way as the solution of any other historical problem.

So far as I know, there are only three hypotheses which ever have been entertained, or which well can be entertained, respecting the past history of Nature. I will, in the first place, state the hypotheses, and then I will consider what evidence bearing upon them is in our possession, and by what light of criticism that evidence is to be interpreted.

Upon the first hypothesis, the assumption is, that phenomena of Nature similar to those exhibited by the present world have always existed;

in other words, that the universe has existed from all eternity in what may be broadly termed its present condition.

The second hypothesis is, that the present state of things has had only a limited duration; and that, at some period in the past, a condition of the world, essentially similar to that which we now know, came into existence, without any precedent condition from which it could have naturally proceeded. The assumption that successive states of Nature have arisen, each without any relation of natural causation to an antecedent state, is a mere modification of this second hypothesis.

The third hypothesis also assumes that the present state of things has had but a limited duration; but it supposes that this state has been evolved by a natural process from an antecedent state, and that from another, and so on; and, on this hypothesis, the attempt to assign any limit to the series of past changes is, usually, given up.

It is so needful to form clear and distinct notions of what is really meant by each of these hypotheses that I will ask you to imagine what, according to each, would have been visible to a spectator of the events which constitute the history of the earth. On the first hypothesis, however far back in time that spectator might be placed, he would see a world essentially, though perhaps not in all its details, similar to that which now exists. The animals which existed would be the ancestors of those which now live, and similar to them; the plants, in like manner, would be such as we know; and the mountains, plains, and waters would foreshadow the salient features of our present land and water. This view was held more or less distinctly, sometimes combined with the notion of recurrent cycles of change, in ancient times; and its influence has been felt down to the present day. It is worthy of remark that it is a hypothesis which is not inconsistent with the doctrine of Uniformitarianism, with which geologists are familiar. That doctrine was held by Hutton, and in his earlier days by Lyell. Hutton was struck by the demonstration of astronomers that the perturbations of the planetary bodies, however great they may be, yet sooner or later right themselves; and that the solar system possesses a self-adjusting power by which these aberrations are all brought back to a mean condition. Hutton imagined that the like might be true of terrestrial changes; although no one recognised more clearly than he the fact that the dry land is being constantly washed down by rain and rivers and deposited in the sea; and that thus, in a longer or shorter time, the inequalities of the earth's surface must be levelled, and its high lands brought down to the ocean. But, taking into account the internal forces of the earth, which, upheaving the sea-bottom give rise to new land, he thought that these operations of degradation and elevation might compensate each other; and that thus, for any assignable time, the general features of our planet might remain what they are. And inasmuch as, under these circumstances, there need be no limit to the propagation of animals and plants, it is clear that the consistent working-out of the uniformitarian idea might lead to the conception of the eternity of the world. Not that I mean to say that either Hutton or Lyell held this conception — assuredly not; they would have been the first to repudiate it. Nevertheless, the logical development of their arguments tends directly towards this hypothesis.

The second hypothesis supposes that the present order of things, at some no very remote time, had a sudden origin, and that the world, such as it now is, had chaos for its phenomenal antecedent. That is the doctrine which you will find stated most fully and clearly in the immortal poem of John Milton — the English *Divina Commedia* — *Paradise Lost*. I believe it is largely to the influence of that remarkable work, combined with the daily teachings to which we have all listened in our childhood, that this hypothesis owes its general wide diffusion as one of the current beliefs of English-speaking people. If you turn to the seventh book of *Paradise Lost*, you will find there stated the hypothesis to which I refer, which is briefly this: That this visible universe of ours came into existence at no great distance of time from the present; and that the parts of which it is composed made their appearance, in a certain definite order, in the space of six natural days, in such a manner that, on the first of these days, light appeared; that, on the second, the firmament, or sky, separated the waters above, from the waters beneath the firmament; that, on the third day, the waters drew away from the dry land, and upon it a varied vegetable life, similar to that which now exists, made its appearance; that the fourth day was signalised by the apparition of the sun, the stars, the moon, and the planets; that, on the fifth day, aquatic animals originated within the waters; that, on the sixth day, the earth gave rise to our four-footed terrestrial creatures, and to all varieties of terrestrial animals except birds, which had appeared on the preceding day; and, finally, that man appeared upon the earth, and the emergence of the universe from chaos was finished. Milton tells us, without the least ambiguity, what a spectator of these marvellous occurrences would have witnessed. I doubt not that his poem is familiar to all of you, but I should like to recall one passage to your minds, in order that I may be justified in what I have said regarding the perfectly concrete, definite picture of the origin of the animal world which Milton draws. He says: —

> "The sixth, and of creation last, arose
> With evening harps and matin, when God said,
> 'Let the earth bring forth soul living in her kind,
> Cattle and creeping things, and beast of the earth,
> Each in their kind!' The earth obeyed, and, straight

Opening her fertile womb, teemed at a birth
Innumerous living creatures, perfect forms,
Limbed and full-grown. Out of the ground uprose,
As from his lair, the wild beast, where he wons
In forest wild, in thicket, brake, or den;
Among the trees in pairs they rose, they walked;
The cattle in the fields and meadows green;
Those rare and solitary; these in flocks
Pasturing at once, and in broad herds upsprung.
The grassy clods now calved; now half appears
The tawny lion, pawing to get free
His hinder parts — then springs, as broke from bonds,
And rampant shakes his brinded mane; the ounce,
The libbard, and the tiger, as the mole
Rising, the crumbled earth above them threw
In hillocks; the swift stag from underground
Bore up his branching head; scarce from his mould
Behemoth, biggest born of earth, upheaved
His vastness; fleeced the flocks and bleating rose
As plants; ambiguous between sea and land,
The river-horse and scaly crocodile.
At once came forth whatever creeps the ground,
Insect or worm."

There is no doubt as to the meaning of this statement, nor as to what a man of Milton's genius expected would have been actually visible to an eye-witness of this mode of origination of living things.

The third hypothesis, or the hypothesis of evolution, supposes that, at any comparatively late period of past time, our imaginary spectator would meet with a state of things very similar to that which now obtains; but that the likeness of the past to the present would gradually become less and less, in proportion to the remoteness of his period of observation from the present day; that the existing distribution of mountains and plains, of rivers and seas, would show itself to be the product of a slow process of natural change operating upon more and more widely different antecedent conditions of the mineral framework of the earth; until, at length, in place of that framework, he would behold only a vast nebulous mass, representing the constituents of the sun and of the planetary bodies. Preceding the forms of life which now exist, our observer would see animals and plants not identical with them, but like them; increasing their differences with their antiquity and, at the same time, becoming simpler and simpler; until, finally, the world of life would present nothing but that undifferentiated protoplasmic matter which, so far as our present knowledge goes, is the common foundation of all vital activity.

The hypothesis of evolution supposes that in all this vast progression there would be no breach of continuity, no point at which we could say "This a natural process," and "This is not a natural process;" but that the whole might be compared to that wonderful process of development which may be seen going on every day under our eyes, in virtue of which there arises, out of the semi-fluid, comparatively homogeneous substance which we call an egg, the complicated organization of one of the higher animals. That, in a few words, is what is meant by the hypothesis of evolution.

I have already suggested that in dealing with these three hypotheses, in endeavouring to form a judgment as to which of them is the more worthy of belief, or whether none is worthy of belief — in which case our condition of mind should be that suspension of judgment which is so difficult to all but trained intellects — we should be indifferent to all *à priori* considerations. The question is a question of historical fact. The universe has come into existence somehow or other, and the problem is, whether it came into existence in one fashion, or whether it came into existence in another; and, as an essential preliminary to further discussion, permit me to say two or three words as to the nature and the kinds of historical evidence.

The evidence as to the occurrence of any event in past time may be ranged under two heads which, for convenience' sake, I will speak of as testimonial evidence and as circumstantial evidence. By testimonial evidence I mean human testimony; and by circumstantial evidence I mean evidence which is not human testimony. Let me illustrate by a familiar example what I understand by these two kinds of evidence, and what is to be said respecting their value.

Suppose that a man tells you that he saw a person strike another and kill him; that is testimonial evidence of the fact of murder. But it is possible to have circumstantial evidence of the fact of murder; that is to say, you may find a man dying with a wound upon his head having exactly the form and character of the wound which is made by an axe, and, with due care in taking surrounding circumstances into account, you may conclude with the utmost certainty that the man has been murdered; that his death is the consequence of a blow inflicted by another man with that implement. We are very much in the habit of considering circumstantial evidence as of less value than testimonial evidence, and it may be that, where the circumstances are not perfectly clear and intelligible, it is a dangerous and unsafe kind of evidence; but it must not be forgotten that, in many cases, circumstantial is quite as conclusive as testimonial evidence, and that, not unfrequently, it is a great deal weightier than testimonial evidence. For example, take the case to which I referred just now. The circumstantial evidence may be better and more convincing than the testimonial evidence; for it may be impossible, under the conditions that I have defined, to suppose that the man met his death from any cause but the violent blow of an axe wielded by another man. The circumstantial evidence in favour of a murder having been committed, in that case, is as complete and as convincing as evidence can be. It is evidence which is open to no doubt and to no falsification. But the testimony of a witness is open to multitudinous doubts. He may have been mistaken. He may have been actuated by malice. It has constantly happened that even an accurate man has declared that a thing has happened in this, that, or the other way, when a careful analysis of the circumstantial evidence has shown that it did not happen in that way, but in some other way.

We may now consider the evidence in favour of or against the three hypotheses. Let me first direct your attention to what is to be said about the hypothesis of the eternity of the state of things in which we now live. What will first strike you is, that it is a hypothesis which, whether true or false, is not capable of verification by any evidence. For, in order to obtain either circumstantial or testimonial evidence sufficient to prove the eternity of duration of the present state of nature, you must have an eternity of witnesses or an infinity of circumstances, and neither of these is attainable. It is utterly impossible that such evidence should be carried beyond a certain point of time; and all that could be said, at most, would be, that so far as the evidence could be traced, there was nothing to contradict the hypothesis. But when you look, not to the testimonial evidence — which, considering the relative insignificance of the antiquity of human records, might not be good for much in this case — but to the circumstantial evidence, then you find that this hypothesis is absolutely incompatible with such evidence as we have; which is of so plain and so simple a character that it is impossible in any way to escape from the conclusions which it forces upon us.

You are, doubtless, all aware that the outer substance of the earth, which alone is accessible to direct observation, is not of a homogeneous character, but that it is made up of a number of layers or strata, the titles of the principal groups of which are placed upon the accompanying diagram. Each of these groups represents a number of beds of sand, of stone, of clay, of slate, and of various other materials.

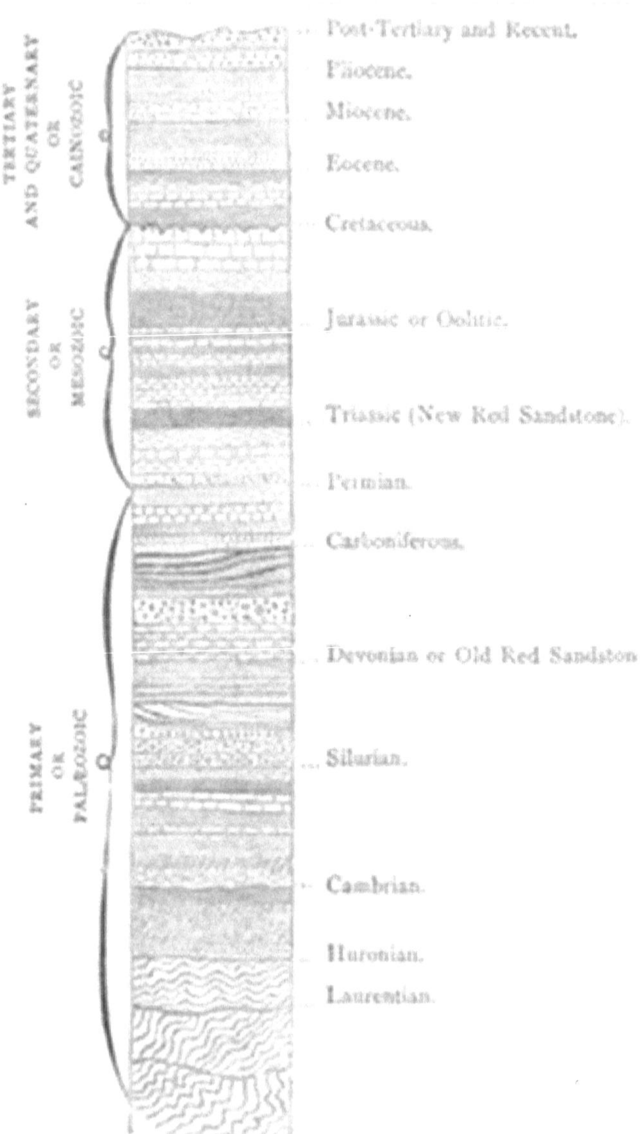

Fig. 1.—Ideal Section of the Crust of the Earth.

On careful examination, it is found that the materials of which each of these layers of more or less hard rock are composed are, for the most part, of the same nature as those which are at present being formed under known conditions on the surface of the earth. For example, the chalk, which constitutes a great part of the Cretaceous formation in some parts of the world, is practically identical in its physical and chemical characters with a substance which is now being formed at the bottom of the Atlantic Ocean, and covers an enormous area; other beds of rock are comparable with the sands which are being formed upon sea-shores, packed together, and so on. Thus, omitting rocks of igneous origin, it is demonstrable that all these beds of stone, of which a total of not less than seventy thousand feet is known, have been formed by natural agencies, either out of the waste and washing of the dry land, or else by the accumulation of the exuviæ of plants and animals. Many of these strata are full of such exuviæ — the so-called "fossils." Remains of thousands of species of animals and plants, as perfectly recognisable as those of existing forms of life which you meet with in museums, or as the shells which you pick up upon the sea-beech, have been imbedded in the ancient sands, or muds, or limestones, just as they are being imbedded now, in sandy, or clayey, or calcareous subaqueous deposits. They furnish us with a record, the general nature of which cannot be misinterpreted, of the kinds of things that have lived upon the surface of the earth during the time that is registered by this great thickness of stratified rocks. But even a superficial study of these fossils shows us that the animals and plants which live at the present time have had only a temporary duration; for the remains of such modern forms of life are met with, for the most part, only in the uppermost or latest tertiaries, and their number rapidly diminishes in the lower deposits of that epoch. In the older tertiaries, the places of existing animals and plants are taken by other forms, as numerous and diversified as those which live now in the same localities, but more or less different from them; in the mesozoic rocks, these are replaced by others yet more divergent from modern types; and in the palæozoic formations the contrast is still more marked. Thus the circumstantial evidence absolutely negatives the conception of the eternity of the present condition of things. We can say with certainty that the present condition of things has existed for a comparatively short period; and that, so far as animal and vegetable nature are concerned, it has been preceded by a different condition. We can pursue this evidence until we reach the lowest of the stratified rocks, in which we lose the indications of life altogether. The hypothesis of the eternity of the present state of nature may therefore be put out of court.

We now come to what I will term Milton's hypothesis — the hypothesis that the present condition of things has endured for a comparatively short time; and, at the commencement of that time, came into existence within the course of six days. I doubt not that it may have excited some surprise in your minds that I should have spoken of this as Milton's hypothesis, rather than that I should have chosen the terms which are more customary, such as "the doctrine of creation," or "the Biblical doctrine," or "the doctrine of Moses," all of which denominations, as applied to the hypothesis to which I have just referred, are certainly much more familiar to you than the title of the Miltonic hypothesis. But I have had what I cannot but think are very weighty reasons for taking the course which I have pursued. In the first place, I have discarded the title of the "doctrine of creation," because my present business is not with the question why the objects which constitute Nature came into existence, but when they came into existence, and in what order. This is as strictly a historical question as the question when the Angles and the Jutes invaded England, and whether they preceded or followed the Romans. But the question about creation is a philosophical problem, and one which cannot be solved, or even approached, by the historical method. What we want to learn is, whether the facts, so far as they are known, afford evidence that things arose in the way described by Milton, or whether they do not; and, when that question is settled, it will be time enough to inquire into the causes of their origination.

In the second place, I have not spoken of this doctrine as the Biblical doctrine. It is quite true that persons as diverse in their general views as Milton the Protestant and the celebrated Jesuit Father Suarez, each put upon the first chapter of Genesis the interpretation embodied in Milton's poem. It is quite true that this interpretation is that which has been instilled into every one of us in our childhood; but I do not for one moment venture to say that it can properly be called the Biblical doctrine. It is not my business, and does not lie within my competency, to say what the Hebrew text does, and what it does not signify; moreover, were I to affirm that this is the Biblical doctrine, I should be met by the authority of many eminent scholars, to say nothing of men of science, who, at various times, have absolutely denied that any such doctrine is to be found in Genesis. If we are to listen to many expositors of no mean authority, we must believe that what seems so clearly defined in Genesis — as if very great pains had been taken that there should be no possibility of mistake — is not the meaning of the text at all. The account is divided into periods that we may make just as long or as short as convenience requires. We are also to understand that it is consistent with the original text to believe that the most complex plants and animals may have been evolved by natural processes, lasting for millions of years, out of structureless rudiments. A person who is not a Hebrew scholar can only stand aside and admire the marvellous flexibility of a language which admits of such diverse interpretations. But assuredly, in the face of such contradictions of authority upon matters respecting which he is incompetent to form any judgment, he will abstain, as I do, from giving any opinion.

In the third place, I have carefully abstained from speaking of this as the Mosaic doctrine, because we are now assured upon the authority of the highest critics, and even of dignitaries of the Church, that there is no evidence that Moses wrote the Book of Genesis, or knew anything about it. You will understand that I give no judgment — it would be an impertinence upon my part to volunteer even a suggestion — upon such a subject. But, that being the state of opinion among the scholars and the clergy, it is well for the unlearned in Hebrew lore, and for the laity, to avoid entangling themselves in such a vexed question. Happily, Milton leaves us no excuse for doubting what he means, and I shall therefore be safe in speaking of the opinion in question as the Miltonic hypothesis.

Now we have to test that hypothesis. For my part, I have no prejudice one way or the other. If there is evidence in favour of this view, I am burdened by no theoretical difficulties in the way of accepting it; but there must be evidence. Scientific men get an awkward habit — no, I won't call it that, for it is a valuable habit — of believing nothing unless there is evidence for it; and they have a way of looking upon belief which is not based upon evidence, not only as illogical, but as immoral. We will, if you please, test this view by the circumstantial evidence alone; for, from what I have said, you will understand that I do not propose to discuss the question of what testimonial evidence is to be adduced in favour of it. If those whose business it is to judge are not at one as to the authenticity of the only evidence of that kind which is offered, nor as to the facts to which it bears witness, the discussion of such evidence is superfluous.

But I may be permitted to regret this necessity of rejecting the testimonal evidence the less, because the examination of the circumstantial evidence leads to the conclusion, not only that it is incompetent to justify the hypothesis, but that, so far as it goes, it is contrary to the hypothesis.

The considerations upon which I base this conclusion are of the simplest possible character. The Miltonic hypothesis contains assertions of a very definite character relating to the succession of living forms. It is stated that plants, for example, made their appearance upon the third day, and not before. And you will understand that what the poet means by plants are such plants as now live, the ancestors, in the ordinary way of propagation of like by like, of the trees and shrubs which flourish in the present world. It must needs be so; for, if they were different, either the existing plants have been the result of a separate origination since that described by Milton, of which we have no record, nor any ground for supposition that such an occurrence has taken place; or else they have arisen by a process of evolution from the original stocks.

In the second place, it is clear that there was no animal life before the fifth day, and that, on the fifth day, aquatic animals and birds appeared. And it is further clear that terrestrial living things, other than birds, made their appearance upon the sixth day, and not before. Hence, it follows that, if, in the large mass of circumstantial evidence as to what really has happened in the past history of the globe we find indications of the existence of terrestrial animals, other than birds, at a certain period, it is perfectly certain that all that has taken place since that time must be referred to the sixth day.

In the great Carboniferous formation, whence America derives so vast a proportion of her actual and potential wealth, in the beds of coal which have been formed from the vegetation of that period, we find abundant evidence of the existence of terrestrial animals. They have been described, not only by European but by your own naturalists. There are to be found numerous insects allied to our cockroaches. There are to be found spiders and scorpions of large size, the latter so similar to existing scorpions that it requires the practised eye of the naturalist to distinguish them. Inasmuch as these animals can be proved to have been alive in the Carboniferous epoch, it is perfectly clear that, if the Miltonic account is to be accepted, the huge mass of rocks extending from the middle of the Palæozoic formations to the uppermost members of the series, must belong to the day which is termed by Milton the sixth. But, further, it is expressly stated that aquatic animals took their origin upon the fifth day, and not before; hence, all formations in which remains of aquatic animals can be proved to exist, and which therefore testify that such animals lived at the time when these formations were in course of deposition, must have been deposited during or since the period which Milton speaks of as the fifth day. But there is absolutely no fossiliferous formation in which the remains of aquatic animals are absent. The oldest fossils in the Silurian rocks are exuviæ of marine animals; and if the view which is entertained by Principal Dawson and Dr. Carpenter respecting the nature of the *Eozoön* be well founded, aquatic animals existed at a period as far antecedent to the deposition of the coal as the coal is from us; inasmuch as the *Eozoön* is met with in those Laurentian strata which lie at the bottom of the series of stratified rocks. Hence it follows, plainly enough, that the whole series of stratified rocks, if they are to be brought into harmony with Milton, must be referred to the fifth and sixth days, and that we cannot hope to find the slightest trace of the products of the earlier days in the geological record. When we consider these simple facts, we see how absolutely futile are the attempts that have been made to draw a parallel between the story told by so much of the crust of the earth as is known to us and the story which Milton tells. The whole series of fossiliferous stratified rocks must be referred to the last two days; and neither the Carboniferous, nor any other, formation can afford evidence of the work of the third day.

Not only is there this objection to any attempt to establish a harmony between the Miltonic account and the facts recorded in the fossiliferous rocks, but there is a further difficulty. According to the Miltonic account, the order in which animals should have made their appearance in the stratified rocks would be this: Fishes, including the great whales, and birds; after them, all varieties of terrestrial animals except birds. Nothing could be further from the facts as we find them; we know of not the slightest evidence of the existence of birds before the Jurassic, or perhaps the Triassic, formation; while terrestrial animals, as we have just seen, occur in the Carboniferous rocks.

If there were any harmony between the Miltonic account and the circumstantial evidence, we ought to have abundant evidence of the existence of birds in the Carboniferous, the Devonian, and the Silurian rocks. I need hardly say that this is not the case, and that not a trace of birds makes its appearance until the far later period which I have mentioned.

And again, if it be true that all varieties of fishes and the great whales, and the like, made their appearance on the fifth day, we ought to find the remains of these animals in the older rocks—in those which were deposited before the Carboniferous epoch. Fishes we do find, in considerable number and variety; but the great whales are absent, and the fishes are not such as now live. Not one solitary species of fish now in existence is to be found in the Devonian or Silurian formations. Hence we are introduced afresh to the dilemma which I have already placed before you: either the animals which came into existence on the fifth day were not such as those which are found at present, are not the direct and immediate ancestors of those which now exist; in which case either fresh creations of which nothing is said; or a process of evolution must have occurred; or else the whole story must be given up, as not only devoid of any circumstantial evidence, but contrary to such evidence as exists.

I placed before you in a few words, some little time ago, a statement of the sum and substance of Milton's hypothesis. Let me now try to state as briefly, the effect of the circumstantial evidence bearing upon the past history of the earth which is furnished, without the possibility of mistake, with no chance of error as to its chief features, by the stratified rocks. What we find is, that the great series of formations represents a period of time of which our human chronologies hardly afford us a unit of measure. I will not pretend to say how we ought to estimate this time, in millions or in billions of years. For my purpose, the determination of its absolute duration is wholly unessential. But that the time was enormous there can be no question.

It results from the simplest methods of interpretation, that leaving out of view certain patches of metamorphosed rocks, and certain volcanic products, all that is now dry land has once been at the bottom of the waters. It is perfectly certain that, at a comparatively recent period of the world's history — the Cretaceous epoch — none of the great physical features which at present mark the surface of the globe existed. It is certain that the Rocky Mountains were not. It is certain that the Himalaya Mountains were not. It is certain that the Alps and the Pyrenees had no existence. The evidence is of the plainest possible character, and is simply this: — We find raised up on the flanks of these mountains, elevated by the forces of upheaval which have given rise to them, masses of Cretaceous rock which formed the bottom of the sea before those mountains existed. It is therefore clear that the elevatory forces which gave rise to the mountains operated subsequently to the Cretaceous epoch; and that the mountains themselves are largely made up of the materials deposited in the sea which once occupied their place. As we go back in time, we meet with constant alternations of sea and land, of estuary and open ocean; and, in correspondence with these alternations, we observe the changes in the fauna and flora to which I have referred.

But the inspection of these changes give us no right to believe that there has been any discontinuity in natural processes. There is no trace of general cataclysms, of universal deluges, or sudden destructions of a whole fauna or flora. The appearances which were formerly interpreted in that way have all been shown to be delusive, as our knowledge has increased and as the blanks which formerly appeared to exist between the different formations have been filled up. That there is no absolute break between formation and formation, that there has been no sudden disappearance of all the forms of life and replacement of them by others, but that changes have gone on slowly and gradually, that one type has died out and another has taken its place, and that thus, by insensible degrees, one fauna has been replaced by another, are conclusions strengthened by constantly increasing evidence. So that within the whole of the immense period indicated by the fossiliferous stratified rocks, there is assuredly not the slightest proof of any break in the uniformity of Nature's operations, no indication that events have followed other than a clear and orderly sequence.

That, I say, is the natural and obvious teaching of the circumstantial evidence contained in the stratified rocks. I leave you to consider how far, by any ingenuity of interpretation, by any stretching of the meaning of language, it can be brought into harmony with the Miltonic hypothesis.

There remains the third hypothesis, that of which I have spoken as the hypothesis of evolution; and I purpose that, in lectures to come, we should discuss it as carefully as we have considered the other two hypotheses. I need not say that it is quite hopeless to look for testimonial evidence of evolution. The very nature of the case precludes the possibility of such evidence, for the human race can no more be expected to testify to its own origin, than a child can be tendered as a witness of its own birth. Our sole inquiry is, what foundation circumstantial evidence lends to the hypothesis, or whether it lends none, or whether it controverts the hypothesis. I shall deal with the matter entirely as a question of history. I shall not indulge in the discussion of any speculative probabilities. I shall not attempt to show that Nature is unintelligible unless we adopt some such hypothesis. For anything I know about the matter, it may be the way of Nature to be unintelligible; she is often puzzling, and I have no reason to suppose that she is bound to fit herself to our notions.

I shall place before you three kinds of evidence entirely based upon what is known of the forms of animal life which are contained in the series of stratified rocks. I shall endeavour to show you that there is one kind of evidence which is neutral, which neither helps evolution nor is inconsistent with it. I shall then bring forward a second kind of evidence which indicates a strong probability in favour of evolution, but does not prove it; and, lastly, I shall adduce a third kind of evidence which, being as complete as any evidence which we can hope to obtain upon such a subject, and being wholly and strikingly in favour of evolution, may fairly be called demonstrative evidence of its occurrence.

LECTURE II
THE HYPOTHESIS OF EVOLUTION.
THE NEUTRAL AND THE
FAVOURABLE EVIDENCE

In the preceding lecture I pointed out that there are three hypotheses which may be entertained, and which have been entertained, respecting the past history of life upon the globe. According to the first of these hypotheses, living beings, such as now exist, have existed from all eternity upon this earth. We tested that hypothesis by the circumstantial evidence, as I called it, which is furnished by the fossil remains contained in the earth's crust, and we found that it was obviously untenable. I then proceeded to consider the second hypothesis, which I termed the Miltonic hypothesis, not because it is of any particular consequence to me whether John Milton seriously entertained it or not, but because it is stated in a clear and unmistakable manner in his great poem. I pointed out to you that the evidence at our command as completely and fully negatives that hypothesis as it did the preceding one. And I confess that I had too much respect for your intelligence to think it necessary to add that the negation was equally clear and equally valid, whatever the source from which that hypothesis might be derived, or whatever the authority by which it might be supported. I further stated that, according to the third hypothesis, or that of evolution, the existing state of things is the last term of a long series of states, which, when traced back, would be found to show no interruption and no breach in the continuity of natural causation. I propose, in the present, and the following lecture, to test this hypothesis rigorously by the evidence at command, and to inquire how far that evidence can be said to be indifferent to it, how far it can be said to be favourable to it, and, finally, how far it can be said to be demonstrative.

From almost the origin of the discussions about the existing condition of the animal and vegetable worlds and the causes which have determined that condition, an argument has been put forward as an objection to evolution, which we shall have to consider very seriously. It is an argument which was first clearly stated by Cuvier in his criticism of the doctrines propounded by his great contemporary, Lamarck. The French expedition to Egypt had called the attention of learned men to the wonderful store of antiquities in that country, and there had been brought back to France numerous mummified corpses of the animals which the ancient Egyptians revered and preserved, and which, at a reasonable computation, must have lived not less than three or four thousand years before the time at which they were thus brought to light. Cuvier endeavoured to test the hypothesis that animals have undergone gradual and progressive modifications of structure, by comparing the skeletons and such other parts of the mummies as were in a fitting state of preservation, with the corresponding parts of the representatives of the same species now living in Egypt. He arrived at the conviction that no appreciable change had taken place in these animals in the course of this considerable lapse of time, and the justice of his conclusion is not disputed.

It is obvious that, if it can be proved that animals have endured, without undergoing any demonstrable change of structure, for so long a period as four thousand years, no form of the hypothesis of evolution which assumes that animals undergo a constant and necessary progressive change can be tenable; unless, indeed, it be further assumed that four thousand years is too short a time for the production of a change sufficiently great to be detected.

But it is no less plain that if the process of evolution of animals is not independent of surrounding conditions; if it may be indefinitely hastened or retarded by variations in these conditions; or if evolution is simply a process of accommodation to varying conditions; the argument against the hypothesis of evolution based on the unchanged character of the Egyptian fauna is worthless. For the monuments which are coeval with the mummies testify as strongly to the absence of change in the physical geography and the general conditions of the land of Egypt, for the time in question, as the mummies do to the unvarying characters of its living population.

The progress of research since Cuvier's time has supplied far more striking examples of the long duration of specific forms of life than those which are furnished by the mummified Ibises and Crocodiles of Egypt. A remarkable case is to be found in your own country, in the neighbourhood of the falls of Niagara. In the immediate vicinity of the whirlpool, and again upon Goat Island, in the superficial deposits which cover the surface of the rocky subsoil in those regions, there are found remains of animals in perfect preservation, and among them, shells belonging to exactly the same species as those which at present inhabit the still waters of Lake Erie. It is evident, from the structure of the country, that these animal remains were deposited in the beds in which they occur at a time when the lake extended over the region in which they are found. This involves the conclusion that they lived and died before the falls had cut their way back through the gorge of Niagara; and, indeed, it has been determined that, when these animals lived, the falls of Niagara must have been at least six miles further down the river than they are at present. Many computations have been made of the rate at which the falls are thus cutting their way back. Those computations have varied greatly, but I believe I am speaking within the bounds of prudence, if I assume that the falls of Niagara have not retreated at a greater pace than about a foot a year. Six miles, speaking roughly, are 30,000 feet; 30,000 feet, at a foot a year, gives 30,000 years; and thus we are fairly justified in concluding that no less a period than this has passed since the shell-fish, whose remains are left in the beds to which I have referred, were living creatures.

But there is still stronger evidence of the long duration of certain types. I have already stated that, as we work our way through the great series of the Tertiary formations, we find many species of animals identical with those which live at the present day, diminishing in numbers, it is true, but still existing, in a certain proportion, in the oldest of the Tertiary rocks. Furthermore, when we examine the rocks of the Cretaceous epoch, we find the remains of some animals which the closest scrutiny cannot show to be, in any important respect, different from those which live at the present time. That is the case with one of the cretaceous lamp-shells (*Terebratula*), which has continued to exist unchanged, or with insignificant variations, down to the present day. Such is the case with the *Globigerinæ*, the skeletons of which, aggregated together, form a large proportion of our English chalk. Those *Globigerinæ* can be traced down to the *Globigerinæ* which live at the surface of the present great oceans, and the remains of which, falling to the bottom of the sea, give rise to a chalky mud. Hence it must be admitted that certain existing species of animals show no distinct sign of modification, or transformation, in the course of a lapse of time as great as that which carries us back to the Cretaceous period; and which, whatever its absolute measure, is certainly vastly greater than thirty thousand years.

There are groups of species so closely allied together that it needs the eye of a naturalist to distinguish them one from another. If we disregard the small differences which separate these forms and consider all the species of such groups as modifications of one type, we shall find that, even among the higher animals, some types have had a marvellous duration. In the chalk, for example, there is found a fish belonging to the highest and the most differentiated group of osseous fishes, which goes by the name of *Beryx*. The remains of that fish are among the most beautiful and well preserved of the fossils found in our English chalk. It can be studied anatomically, so far as the hard parts are concerned, almost as well as if it were a recent fish.

But the genus *Beryx* is represented, at the present day, by very closely allied species which are living in the Pacific and Atlantic Oceans. We may go still farther back. I have already referred to the fact that the Carboniferous formations, in Europe and in America, contain the remains of scorpions in an admirable state of preservation, and that those scorpions are hardly distinguishable from such as now live. I do not mean to say that they are not different, but close scrutiny is needed in order to distinguish them from modern scorpions.

More than this. At the very bottom of the Silurian series, in beds which are by some authorities referred to the Cambrian formation, where the signs of life begin to fail us — even there, among the few and scanty animal remains which are discoverable, we find species of molluscous animals which are so closely allied to existing forms that, at one time, they were grouped under the same generic name. I refer to the well-known *Lingula* of the *Lingula* flags, lately, in consequence of some slight differences, placed in the new genus *Lingulella*. Practically, it belongs to the same great generic group as the *Lingula*, which is to be found at the present day upon your own shores and those of many other parts of the world.

The same truth is exemplified if we turn to certain great periods of the earth's history — as, for example, the Mesozoic epoch. There are groups of reptiles, such as the *Ichthyosauria* and the *Plesiosauria*, which appear shortly after the commencement of this epoch, and they occur in vast numbers. They disappear with the chalk and, throughout the whole of the great series of Mesozoic rocks, they present no such modifications as can safely be considered evidence of progressive modification.

Facts of this kind are undoubtedly fatal to any form of the doctrine of evolution which postulates the supposition that there is an intrinsic necessity, on the part of animal forms which have once come into existence, to undergo continual modification; and they are as distinctly opposed to any view which involves the belief, that such modification as may occur, must take place, at the same rate, in all the different types of animal or vegetable life. The facts, as I have placed them before you, obviously directly contradict any form of the hypothesis of evolution which stands in need of these two postulates.

But, one great service that has been rendered by Mr. Darwin to the doctrine of evolution in general is this: he has shown that there are two chief factors in the process of evolution: one of them is the tendency to vary, the existence of which in all living forms may be proved by observation; the other is the influence of surrounding conditions upon what I may call the parent form and the variations which are thus evolved from it. The cause of the production of variations is a matter not at all properly understood

at present. Whether variation depends upon some intricate machinery —
if I may use the phrase — of the living organism itself, or whether it arises
through the influence of conditions upon that form, is not certain, and the
question may, for the present, be left open. But the important point is that,
granting the existence of the tendency to the production of variations; then,
whether the variations which are produced shall survive and supplant the
parent, or whether the parent form shall survive and supplant the variations,
is a matter which depends entirely on those conditions which give rise to
the struggle for existence. If the surrounding conditions are such that the
parent form is more competent to deal with them and flourish in them, than
the derived forms, then, in the struggle for existence, the parent form will
maintain itself and the derived forms will be exterminated. But if, on the
contrary, the conditions are such as to be more favourable to a derived than
to the parent form, the parent form will be extirpated and the derived form
will take its place. In the first case, there will be no progression, no change of
structure, through any imaginable series of ages; in the second place, there
will be modification and change of form.

Thus the existence of these persistent types, as I have termed them, is
no real obstacle in the way of the theory of evolution. Take the case of the
scorpions to which I have just referred. No doubt, since the Carboniferous
epoch, conditions have always obtained, such as existed when the scorpions
of that epoch flourished; conditions in which scorpions find themselves
better off, more competent to deal with the difficulties in their way, than any
variation from the scorpion type which they may have produced; and, for
that reason, the scorpion type has persisted, and has not been supplanted
by any other form. And there is no reason, in the nature of things, why, as
long as this world exists, if there be conditions more favourable to scorpions
than to any variation which may arise from them, these forms of life should
not persist.

Therefore, the stock objection to the hypothesis of evolution, based on
the long duration of certain animal and vegetable types, is no objection at
all. The facts of this character — and they are numerous — belong to that class
of evidence which I have called indifferent. That is to say, they may afford
no direct support to the doctrine of evolution, but they are capable of being
interpreted in perfect consistency with it.

There is another order of facts belonging to the class of negative or
indifferent evidence. The great group of Lizards, which abound in the

present world, extends through the whole series of formations as far back as the Permian, or latest Palæozoic, epoch. These Permian lizards differ astonishingly little from the lizards which exist at the present day. Comparing the amount of the differences between them and modern lizards, with the prodigious lapse of time between the Permian epoch and the present age, it may be said that the amount of change is insignificant. But, when we carry our researches farther back in time, we find no trace of lizards, nor of any true reptile whatever, in the whole mass of formations beneath the Permian.

Now, it is perfectly clear that if our palæontological collections are to be taken, even approximately, as an adequate representation of all the forms of animals and plants that have ever lived; and if the record furnished by the known series of beds of stratified rock, covers the whole series of events which constitute the history of life on the globe, such a fact as this directly contravenes the hypothesis of evolution; because this hypothesis postulates that the existence of every form must have been preceded by that of some form little different from it. Here, however, we have to take into consideration that important truth so well insisted upon by Lyell and by Darwin—the imperfection of the geological record. It can be demonstrated that the geological record must be incomplete, that it can only preserve remains found in certain favourable localities and under particular conditions; that it must be destroyed by processes of denudation, and obliterated by processes of metamorphosis. Beds of rock of any thickness, crammed full of organic remains, may yet, either by the percolation of water through them, or by the influence of subterranean heat, lose all trace of these remains, and present the appearance of beds of rock formed under conditions in which living forms were absent. Such metamorphic rocks occur in formations of all ages; and, in various cases, there are very good grounds for the belief that they have contained organic remains, and that those remains have been absolutely obliterated.

I insist upon the defects of the geological record the more because those who have not attended to these matters are apt to say, "It is all very well, but when you get into a difficulty with your theory of evolution, you appeal to the incompleteness and the imperfection of the geological record;" and I want to make it perfectly clear to you that this imperfection is a great fact, which must be taken into account in all our speculations, or we shall constantly be going wrong.

Fig. 2.—Tracks of Brontozoum.

You see the singular series of footmarks, drawn of its natural size in the large diagram hanging up here (Fig. 2), which I owe to the kindness of my friend Professor Marsh, with whom I had the opportunity recently of visiting the precise locality in Massachusetts in which these tracks occur. I am, therefore, able to give you my own testimony, if needed, that the diagram accurately represents what we saw. The valley of the Connecticut is classical ground for the geologist. It contains great beds of sandstone, covering many square miles, which have evidently formed a part of an ancient sea-shore, or, it may be, lake-shore. For a certain period of time after their deposition, these beds have remained sufficiently soft to receive the impressions of the feet of whatever animals walked over them, and to preserve them afterwards, in exactly the same way as such impressions are at this hour preserved on the shores of the Bay of Fundy and elsewhere. The diagram represents the track of some gigantic animal, which walked on its hind legs. You see the series of marks made alternately by the right and by the left foot; so that, from one impression to the other of the three-toed foot on the same side, is one stride, and that stride, as we measured it, is six feet nine inches. I leave you, therefore, to form an impression of the magnitude of the creature which, as it walked along the ancient shore, made these impressions.

Of such impressions there are untold thousands upon these sandstones. Fifty or sixty different kinds have been discovered, and they cover vast areas. But, up to this present time, not a bone, not a fragment, of any one of the animals which left these great footmarks has been found; in fact, the only animal remains which have been met with in all these deposits, from the time of their discovery to the present day — though they have been carefully hunted over — is a fragmentary skeleton of one of the smaller forms. What has become of the bones of all these animals? You see we are not dealing with little creatures, but with animals that make a step of six feet nine inches; and their remains must have been left somewhere. The probability is, that they been dissolved away, and absolutely lost.

I have had occasion to work out the nature of fossil remains, of which there was nothing left except casts of the bones, the solid material of the skeleton having been dissolved out by percolating water. It was a chance, in this case, that the sandstone happened to be of such a constitution as to set, and to allow the bones to be afterward dissolved out, leaving cavities of the exact shape of the bones. Had that constitution been other than what it was, the bones would have been dissolved, the layers of sandstone would have fallen together into one mass, and not the slightest indication that the animal had existed would have been discoverable.

I know of no more striking evidence than these facts afford, of the caution which should be used in drawing the conclusion, from the absence of organic remains in a deposit, that animals or plants did not exist at the time it was formed. I believe that, with a right understanding of the doctrine of evolution on the one hand, and a just estimation of the importance of the imperfection of the geological record on the other, all difficulty is removed from the kind of evidence to which I have adverted; and that we are justified in believing that all such cases are examples of what I have designated negative or indifferent evidence—that is to say, they in no way directly advance the hypothesis of evolution, but they are not to be regarded as obstacles in the way of our belief in that doctrine.

I now pass on to the consideration of those cases which, for reasons which I will point out to you by and by, are not to be regarded as demonstrative of the truth of evolution, but which are such as must exist if evolution be true, and which therefore are, upon the whole, evidence in favour of the doctrine. If the doctrine of evolution be true, it follows, that, however diverse the different groups of animals and of plants may be, they must all, at one time or other, have been connected by gradational forms; so that, from the highest animals, whatever they may be, down to the lowest speck of protoplasmic matter in which life can be manifested, a series of gradations, leading from one end of the series to the other, either exists or has existed. Undoubtedly that is a necessary postulate of the doctrine of evolution. But when we look upon living Nature as it is, we find a totally different state of things. We find that animals and plants fall into groups, the different members of which are pretty closely allied together, but which are separated by definite, larger or smaller, breaks from other groups. In other words, no intermediate forms which bridge over these gaps or intervals are, at present, to be met with.

To illustrate what I mean: Let me call your attention to those vertebrate animals which are most familiar to you, such as mammals, birds, and reptiles. At the present day, these groups of animals are perfectly well defined from one another. We know of no animal now living which, in any sense, is intermediate between the mammal and the bird, or between the bird and the reptile; but, on the contrary, there are many very distinct anatomical peculiarities, well-defined marks, by which the mammal is separated from the bird, and the bird from the reptile. The distinctions are obvious and striking if you compare the definitions of these great groups as they now exist.

The same may be said of many of the subordinate groups, or orders, into which these great classes are divided. At the present time, for example, there are numerous forms of non-ruminant pachyderms, or what we may call broadly, the pig tribe, and many varieties of ruminants. These latter have their definite characteristics, and the former have their distinguishing peculiarities. But there is nothing that fills up the gap between the ruminants and the pig tribe. The two are distinct. Such also is the case in respect of the minor groups of the class of reptiles. The existing fauna shows us crocodiles, lizards, snakes, and tortoises; but no connecting link between the crocodile and lizard, nor between the lizard and snake, nor between the snake and the crocodile, nor between any two of these groups. They are separated by absolute breaks. If, then, it could be shown that this state of things had always existed, the fact would be fatal to the doctrine of evolution. If the intermediate gradations, which the doctrine of evolution requires to have existed between these groups, are not to be found anywhere in the records of the past history of the globe, their absence is a strong and weighty negative argument against evolution; while, on the other hand, if such intermediate forms are to be found, that is so much to the good of evolution; although, for reasons which I will lay before you by and by, we must be cautious in our estimate of the evidential cogency of facts of this kind.

It is a very remarkable circumstance that, from the commencement of the serious study of fossil remains; in fact, from the time when Cuvier began his brilliant researches upon those found in the quarries of Montmartre, palæontology has shown what she was going to do in this matter, and what kind of evidence it lay in her power to produce.

I said just now that, in the existing Fauna, the group of pig-like animals and the group of ruminants are entirely distinct; but one of the first of Cuvier's discoveries was an animal which he called the *Anoplotherium*, and which proved to be, in a great many important respects, intermediate in character between the pigs, on the one hand, and the ruminants on the other. Thus research into the history of the past did, to a certain extent, tend to fill up the breach between the group of ruminants and the group of pigs. Another remarkable animal restored by the great French palæontologist, the *Palæotherium*, similarly tended to connect together animals to all appearance so different as the rhinoceros, the horse, and the tapir. Subsequent research has brought to light multitudes of facts of the same order; and, at the present day, the investigations of such anatomists as Rütimeyer and Gaudry have tended to fill up, more and more, the gaps in our existing series of mammals, and to connect groups formerly thought to be distinct.

But I think it may have an especial interest if, instead of dealing with these examples, which would require a great deal of tedious osteological detail, I take the case of birds and reptiles; groups which, at the present day, are so clearly distinguished from one another that there are perhaps no classes of animals which, in popular apprehension, are more completely separated. Existing birds, as you are aware, are covered with feathers; their anterior extremities, specially and peculiarly modified, are converted into wings, by the aid of which most of them are able to fly; they walk upright upon two legs; and these limbs, when they are considered anatomically, present a great number of exceedingly remarkable peculiarities, to which I may have occasion to advert incidentally as I go on, and which are not met with, even approximately, in any existing forms of reptiles. On the other hand, existing reptiles have no feathers. They may have naked skins, or be covered with horny scales, or bony plates, or with both. They possess no wings; they neither fly by means of their fore-limbs, nor habitually walk upright upon their hind-limbs; and the bones of their legs present no such modifications as we find in birds. It is impossible to imagine any two groups more definitely and distinctly separated, notwithstanding certain characters which they possess in common.

As we trace the history of birds back in time, we find their remains, sometimes in great abundance, throughout the whole extent of the tertiary rocks; but, so far as our present knowledge goes, the birds of the tertiary rocks retain the same essential characters as the birds of the present day. In other words, the tertiary birds come within the definition of the class constituted by existing birds, and are as much separated from reptiles as existing birds are. Not very long ago no remains of birds had been found below the tertiary rocks, and I am not sure but that some persons were prepared to demonstrate that they could not have existed at an earlier period. But in the course of the last few years, such remains have been discovered in England; though, unfortunately, in so imperfect and fragmentary a condition, that it is impossible to say whether they differed from existing birds in any essential character or not. In your country the development of the cretaceous series of rocks is enormous; the conditions under which the later cretaceous strata have been deposited are highly favourable to the preservation of organic remains; and the researches, full of labour and risk, which have been carried on by Professor Marsh in these cretaceous rocks of

Western America, have rewarded him with the discovery of forms of birds of which we had hitherto no conception. By his kindness, I am enabled to place before you a restoration of one of these extraordinary birds, every part of which can be thoroughly justified by the more or less complete skeletons, in a very perfect state of preservation, which he has discovered. This *Hesperornis* (Fig. 3), which measured between five and six feet in length, is astonishingly like our existing divers or grebes in a great many respects; so like them indeed that, had the skeleton of *Hesperornis* been found in a museum without its skull, it probably would have been placed in the same group of birds as the divers and grebes of the present day.[1]

Fig. 3.—Hesperornis Regalis (Marsh).

But *Hesperornis* differs from all existing birds, and so far resembles reptiles, in one important particular—it is provided with teeth. The long jaws are armed with teeth which have curved crowns and thick roots (Fig. 4), and are not set in distinct sockets, but are lodged in a groove. In possessing true teeth, the *Hesperornis* differs from every existing bird, and from every bird yet discovered in the tertiary formations, the tooth-like serrations of the jaws in the *Odontopteryx* of the London clay being mere processes of the bony substance of the jaws, and not teeth in the proper sense of the word. In view of the characteristics of this bird we are therefore obliged to modify the definitions of the classes of birds and reptiles. Before the discovery of *Hesperornis*, the definition of the class Aves based upon our knowledge of existing birds, might have been extended to all birds; it might have been said that the absence of teeth was characteristic of the class of birds; but the discovery of an animal which, in every part of its skeleton, closely agrees with existing birds, and yet possesses teeth, shows that there were ancient birds which, in respect of possessing teeth, approached reptiles more nearly than any existing bird does, and, to that extent, diminishes the *hiatus* between the two classes.

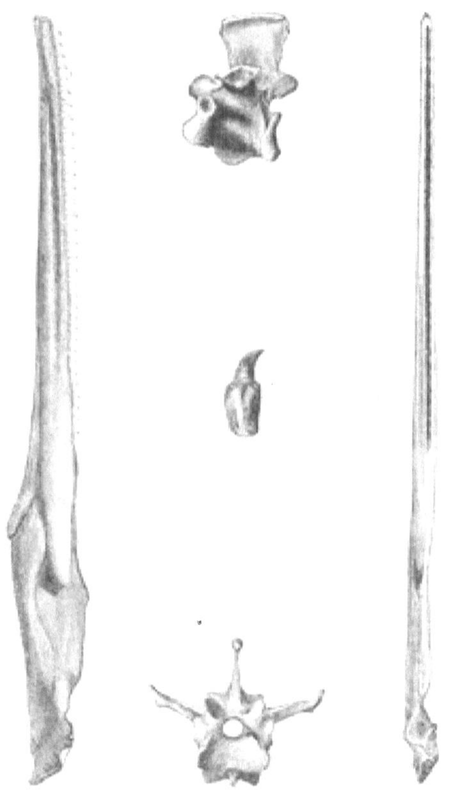

Fig. 4.—Hesperornis Regalis (Marsh).
(Side and upper views of half the lower jaw; side and
end views of a vertebra and a separate tooth.)

The same formation has yielded another bird *Ichthyornis* (Fig. 5), which also possesses teeth; but the teeth are situated in distinct sockets, while those of *Hesperornis* are not so lodged. The latter also has such very small, almost rudimentary, wings, that it must have been chiefly a swimmer and a diver, like a Penguin; while *Ichthyornis* has strong wings and no doubt possessed corresponding powers of flight. *Ichthyornis* also differed in the fact that its vertebræ have not the peculiar characters of the vertebræ of existing and of all known tertiary birds, but were concave at each end. This discovery leads us to make a further modification in the definition of the group of birds, and to part with another of the characters by which almost all existing birds are distinguished from reptiles.

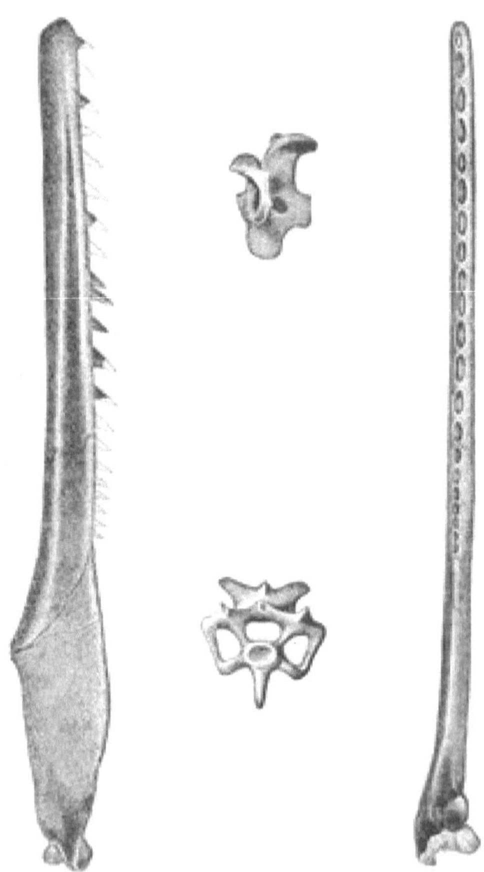

Fig. 5.—Ichthyornis Dispar (Marsh).
(Side and upper views of half the lower jaw; and
side and end views of a vertebra.)

Apart from the few fragmentary remains from the English greensand, to which I have referred, the mesozoic rocks, older than those in which *Hesperornis* and *Ichthyornis* have been discovered have afforded no certain evidence of birds, with the remarkable exception of the Solenhofen slates. These so-called slates are composed of a fine grained calcareous mud which has hardened into lithographic stone, and in which organic remains are almost as well preserved as they would be if they had been imbedded in so much plaster of Paris. They have yielded the *Archæopteryx*, the existence of which was first made known by the finding of a fossil feather, or rather of the impression of one. It is wonderful enough that such a perishable thing as a feather, and nothing more, should be discovered; yet, for a long time, nothing was known of this bird except its feather. But, by and by a solitary skeleton was discovered, which is now in the British Museum. The skull of this solitary specimen is unfortunately wanting, and it is therefore uncertain whether the *Archæopteryx* possessed teeth or not. But the remainder of the skeleton is so well preserved as to leave no doubt respecting the main features of the animal, which are very singular. The feet are not only altogether bird-like, but have the special characters of the feet of perching birds, while the body had a clothing of true feathers. Nevertheless, in some other respects, *Archæopteryx* is unlike a bird and like a reptile. There is a long tail composed of many vertebræ. The structure of the wing differs in some very remarkable respects from that which it presents in a true bird. In the latter, the end of the wing answers to the thumb and two fingers of my hand; but the metacarpal bones, or those which answer to the bones of the fingers which lie in the palm of the hand, are fused together into one mass; and the whole apparatus, except the last joints of the thumb, is bound up in a sheath of integument, while the edge of the hand carries the principal quill-feathers. In the *Archæopteryx*, the upper-arm bone is like that of a bird; and the two bones of the fore-arm are more or less like those of a bird, but the fingers are not bound together—they are free. What their number may have been is uncertain; but several, if not all, of them were terminated by strong curved claws, not like such as are sometimes found in birds, but such as reptiles possess; so that, in the *Archæopteryx*, we have an animal which, to a certain extent, occupies a midway place between a bird and a reptile. It is a bird so far as its foot and sundry other parts of its skeleton are concerned; it is essentially and thoroughly a bird by its feathers; but it is much more properly a reptile in the fact that the region which represents the hand has separate bones, with claws resembling those which terminate the fore-limb of a reptile. Moreover, it had a long reptile-like tail with a fringe of feathers on each side; while, in all true birds hitherto known, the tail is relatively short, and the vertebræ which constitute its skeleton are generally peculiarly modified.

Like the *Anoplotherium* and the *Palæotherium*, therefore, *Archæopteryx* tends to fill up the interval between groups which, in the existing world, are widely separated, and to destroy the value of the definitions of zoological groups based upon our knowledge of existing forms. And such cases as these constitute evidence in favour of evolution, in so far as they prove that, in former periods of the world's history, there were animals which overstepped the bounds of existing groups, and tended to merge them into larger assemblages. They show that animal organisation is more flexible than our knowledge of recent forms might have led us to believe; and that many structural permutations and combinations, of which the present world gives us no indication, may nevertheless have existed.

But it by no means follows, because the *Palæotherium* has much in common with the Horse, on the one hand, and with the Rhinoceros on the other, that it is the intermediate form through which Rhinoceroses have passed to become Horses, or *vice versâ*; on the contrary, any such supposition would certainly be erroneous. Nor do I think it likely that the transition from the reptile to the bird has been effected by such a form as *Archæopteryx*. And it is convenient to distinguish these intermediate forms between two groups, which do not represent the actual passage from the one group to the other, as *intercalary* types, from those *linear* types which, more or less approximately, indicate the nature of the steps by which the transition from one group to the other was effected.

I conceive that such linear forms, constituting a series of natural gradations between the reptile and the bird, and enabling us to understand the manner in which the reptilian has been metamorphosed into the bird type, are really to be found among a group of ancient and extinct terrestrial reptiles known as the *Ornithoscelida*. The remains of these animals occur throughout the series of mesozoic formations, from the Trias to the Chalk, and there are indications of their existence even in the later Palæozoic strata.

Most of these reptiles at present known are of great size, some having attained a length of forty feet or perhaps more. The majority resembled lizards and crocodiles in their general form, and many of them were, like crocodiles, protected by an armour of heavy bony plates. But, in others, the hind limbs elongate and the fore limbs shorten, until their relative proportions approach those which are observed in the short-winged, flightless, ostrich tribe among birds.

The skull is relatively light, and in some cases the jaws, though bearing teeth, are beak-like at their extremities and appear to have been enveloped in a horny sheath. In the part of the vertebral column which lies between the haunch bones and is called the sacrum, a number of vertebræ may unite together into one whole, and in this respect, as in some details of its structure, the sacrum of these reptiles approaches that of birds.

But it is in the structure of the pelvis and of the hind limb that some of these ancient reptiles present the most remarkable approximation to birds, and clearly indicate the way by which the most specialized and characteristic features of the bird may have been evolved from the corresponding parts in the reptile.

In Fig. 6, the pelvis and hind limbs of a crocodile, a three-toed bird, and an ornithoscelidan are represented side by side; and, for facility of comparison, in corresponding positions; but it must be recollected that, while the position of the bird's limb is natural, that of the crocodile is not so. In the bird, the thigh-bone lies close to the body, and the metatarsal bones of the foot (ii., iii., iv., Fig. 6) are, ordinarily, raised into a more or less vertical position; in the crocodile, the thigh-bone stands out at an angle from the body, and the metatarsal bones (i., ii., iii., iv., Fig. 6) lie flat on the ground. Hence, in the crocodile, the body usually lies squat between the legs, while, in the bird, it is raised upon the hind legs, as upon pillars.

In the crocodile, the pelvis is obviously composed of three bones on each side: the ilium (*Il.*), the pubis (*Pb.*), and the ischium (*Is.*). In the adult bird there appears to be but one bone on each side. The examination of the pelvis of a chick, however, shows that each half is made up of three bones, which answer to those which remain distinct throughout life, in the crocodile. There is, therefore, a fundamental identity of plan in the construction of the pelvis of both bird and reptile; though the differences in form, relative size, and direction of the corresponding bones in the two cases are very great.

But the most striking contrast between the two lies in the bones of the leg and of that part of the foot termed the tarsus, which follows upon the leg. In the crocodile, the fibula (*F*) is relatively large and its lower end is complete. The tibia (*T*) has no marked crest at its upper end, and its lower end is narrow and not pulley-shaped. There are two rows of separate tarsal bones (*As.*, *Ca.*, *&c.*) and four distinct metatarsal bones, with a rudiment of a fifth.

In the bird, the fibula is small and its lower end diminishes to a point. The tibia has a strong crest at its upper end and its lower extremity passes into a broad pulley. There seem at first to be no tarsal bones; and only one bone, divided at the end into three heads for the three toes which are attached to it, appears in the place of the metatarsus.

In a young bird, however, the pulley-shaped apparent end of the tibia is a distinct bone, which represents the bones marked *As.*, *Ca.*, in the crocodile; while the apparently single metatarsal bone consists of three bones, which early unite with one another and with an additional bone, which represents the lower row of bones in the tarsus of the crocodile.

In other words, it can be shown by the study of development that the bird's pelvis and hind limb are simply extreme modifications of the same fundamental plan as that upon which these parts are modelled in reptiles.

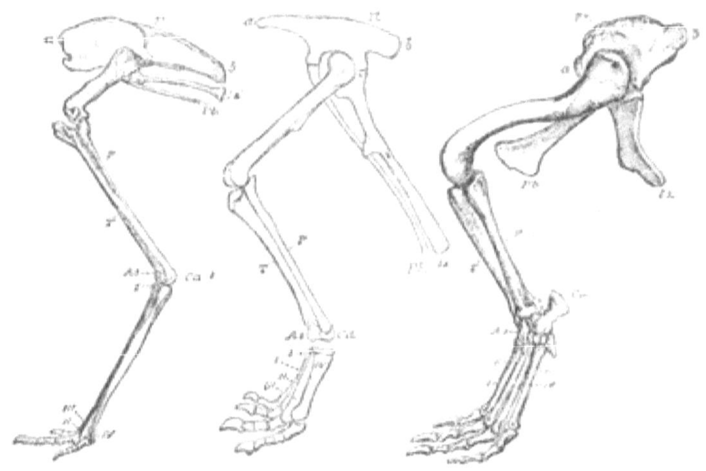

Fig. 6.—Bird. Ornithoscelidan. Crocodile.
(The letters have the same signification in all the figures. *Il.*,
Ilium; *a*, **anterior end;** *b*, **posterior end;** *Is.*, **ischium;** *Pb.*, **pubis;** *T*,
tibia; *F*, **fibula;** *As.*, **astragalus;** *Ca.*, **calcaneum; 1, distal**
portion of the tarsus; i., ii., iii., iv.; metatarsal bones.)

On comparing the pelvis and hind limb of the ornithoscelidan with that of the crocodile, on the one side, and that of the bird, on the other (Fig. 6), it is obvious that it represents a middle term between the two. The pelvic bones approach the form of those of the birds, and the direction of the pubis and ischium is nearly that which is characteristic of birds; the thigh bone, from the direction of its head, must have lain close to the body; the tibia has a great crest; and, immovably fitted on to its lower end, there is a pulley-shaped bone, like that of the bird, but remaining distinct. The lower end of the fibula is much more slender, proportionally, than in the crocodile. The metatarsal bones have such a form that they fit together immovably, though they do not enter into bony union; the third toe is, as in the bird, longest and strongest. In fact, the ornithoscelidan limb is comparable to that of an unhatched chick.

Taking all these facts together, it is obvious that the view, which was entertained by Mantell and the probability of which was demonstrated by your own distinguished anatomist, Leidy, while much additional evidence in the same direction has been furnished by Professor Cope, that some of these animals may have walked upon their hind legs, as birds do, acquires great weight. In fact, there can be no reasonable doubt that one of the smaller forms of the *Ornithoscelida, Compsognathus*, the almost entire skeleton of which has been discovered in the Solenhofen slates, was a bipedal animal. The parts of this skeleton are somewhat twisted out of their natural relations, but the accompanying figure gives a just view of the general form of *Compsognathus* and of the proportions of its limbs; which, in some respects, are more completely bird-like than those of other *Ornithoscelida*.

Fig. 7.—Restoration of Compsognathus Longipes.

We have had to stretch the definition of the class of birds so as to include birds with teeth and birds with paw-like fore-limbs and long tails. There is no evidence that *Compsognathus* possessed feathers; but, if it did, it would be hard indeed to say whether it should be called a reptilian bird or an avian reptile.

As *Compsognathus* walked upon its hind legs, it must have made tracks like those of birds. And as the structure of the limbs of several of the gigantic *Ornithoscelida*, such as *Iguandon*, leads to the conclusion that they also may have constantly, or occasionally, assumed the same attitude, a peculiar interest attaches to the fact that, in the Wealden strata of England, there are to be found gigantic footsteps, arranged in order like those of the *Brontozoum*, and which there can be no reasonable doubt were made by some of the *Ornithoscelida*, the remains of which are found in the same rocks. And, knowing that reptiles that walked upon their hind legs and shared many of the anatomical characters of birds did once exist, it becomes a very important question whether the tracks in the Trias of Massachusetts, to which I referred some time ago, and which formerly used to be unhesitatingly ascribed to birds, may not all have been made by Ornithoscelidan reptiles; and whether, if we could obtain the skeletons of the animals which made these tracks, we should not find in them the actual steps of the evolutional process by which reptiles gave rise to birds.

The evidential value of the facts I have brought forward in this Lecture must be neither over nor under estimated. It is not historical proof of the occurrence of the evolution of birds from reptiles, for we have no safe ground for assuming that true birds had not made their appearance at the commencement of the Mesozoic epoch. It is, in fact, quite possible that all these more or less avi-form reptiles of the Mesozoic epoch are not terms in the series of progression from birds to reptiles at all but simply the more or less modified descendants of Palæozoic forms through which that transition was actually effected.

We are not in a position to say that the known *Ornithoscelida* are intermediate in the order of their appearance on the earth between reptiles and birds. All that can be said is that, if independent evidence of the actual occurrence of evolution is producible, then these intercalary forms remove every difficulty in the way of understanding what the actual steps of the process, in the case of birds, may have been.

That intercalary forms should have existed in ancient times is a necessary consequence of the truth of the hypothesis of evolution; and, hence, the evidence I have laid before you in proof of the existence of such forms, is, so far as it goes, in favour of that hypothesis.

There is another series of extinct reptiles, which may be said to be intercalary between reptiles and birds, in so far as they combine some of the characters of both these groups; and, which, as they possessed the power of flight, may seem, at first sight, to be nearer representatives of the forms by which the transition from the reptile to the bird was effected, than the *Ornithoscelida*.

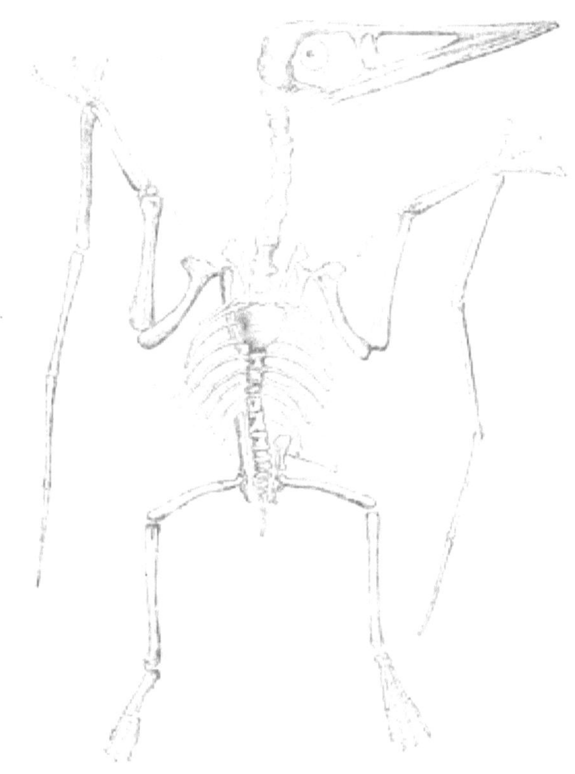

Fig. 8.—Pterodactylus Spectabilis (Von Meyer).

These are the *Pterosauria*, or Pterodactyles, the remains of which are met with throughout the series of Mesozoic rocks, from the lias to the chalk, and some of which attained a great size, their wings having a span of eighteen or twenty feet. These animals, in the form and proportions of the head and neck relatively to the body, and in the fact that the ends of the jaws were often, if not always, more or less extensively ensheathed in horny beaks, remind us of birds. Moreover, their bones contained air cavities, rendering them specifically lighter, as is the case in most birds. The breastbone was large and keeled, as in most birds and in bats, and the shoulder girdle is strikingly similar to that of ordinary birds. But, it seems to me, that the special resemblance of pterodactyles to birds ends here, unless I may add the entire absence of teeth which characterizes the great pterodactyles (*Pteranodon*), discovered by Professor Marsh. All other known pterodactyles have teeth lodged in sockets. In the vertebral column and the hind limbs there are no special resemblances to birds, and when we turn to the wings they are found to be constructed on a totally different principle from those of birds.

There are four fingers. These four fingers are large, and three of them, those which answer to the thumb and two following fingers in my hand — are terminated by claws, while the fourth is enormously prolonged and converted into a great jointed style. You see at once, from what I have stated about a bird's wing, that there could be nothing less like a bird's wing than this is. It concluded by general reasoning that this finger had the office of supporting a web which extended between it and the body. An existing specimen proves that such was really the case, and that the pterodactyles were devoid of feathers, but that the fingers supported a vast web like that of a bat's wing; in fact, there can be no doubt that this ancient reptile flew after the fashion of a bat.

Thus though the pterodactyle is a reptile which has become modified in such a manner as to enable it to fly, and therefore, as might be expected, presents some points of resemblance to other animals which fly; it has, so to speak, gone off the line which leads directly from reptiles to birds, and has become disqualified for the changes which lead to the characteristic organization of the latter class. Therefore, viewed in relation to the classes of reptiles and birds, the pterodactyles appear to me to be, in a limited sense, intercalary forms; but they are not even approximately linear, in the sense of exemplifying those modifications of structure through which the passage from the reptile to the bird took place.

LECTURE III
THE DEMONSTRATIVE
EVIDENCE OF EVOLUTION

The occurrence of historical facts is said to be demonstrated, when the evidence that they happened is of such a character as to render the assumption that they did not happen in the highest degree improbable; and the question I now have to deal with is, whether evidence in favour of the evolution of animals of this degree of cogency is, or is not, obtainable from the record of the succession of living forms which is presented to us by fossil remains.

Those who have attended to the progress of palæontology are aware that evidence of the character which I have defined has been produced in considerable and continually-increasing quantity during the last few years. Indeed, the amount and the satisfactory nature of that evidence are somewhat surprising, when we consider the conditions under which alone we can hope to obtain it.

It is obviously useless to seek for such evidence except in localities in which the physical conditions have been such as to permit of the deposit of an unbroken, or but rarely interrupted, series of strata through a long period of time; in which the group of animals to be investigated has existed in such abundance as to furnish the requisite supply of remains; and in which, finally, the materials composing the strata are such as to ensure the preservation of these remains in a tolerably perfect and undisturbed state.

It so happens that the case which, at present, most nearly fulfils all these conditions is that of the series of extinct animals which culminates in the Horses; by which term I mean to denote not merely the domestic animals with which we are all so well acquainted, but their allies, the ass, zebra, quagga, and the like. In short, I use "horses" as the equivalent of the technical name *Equidæ*, which is applied to the whole group of existing equine animals.

The horse is in many ways a remarkable animal; not least so in the fact that it presents us with an example of one of the most perfect pieces of machinery in the living world. In truth, among the works of human ingenuity it cannot be said that there is any locomotive so perfectly adapted to its purposes, doing so much work with so small a quantity of fuel, as this machine of nature's manufacture — the horse. And, as a necessary consequence of any sort of perfection, of mechanical perfection as of others, you find that the horse is a beautiful creature, one of the most beautiful of all land-animals. Look at the perfect balance of its form, and the rhythm and force of its action. The locomotive machinery is, as you are aware, resident in its slender fore and hind limbs; they are flexible and elastic levers, capable of being moved by very powerful muscles; and, in order to supply the engines which work these levers with the force which they expend, the horse is provided with a very perfect apparatus for grinding its food and extracting therefrom the requisite fuel.

Without attempting to take you very far into the region of osteological detail, I must nevertheless trouble you with some statements respecting the anatomical structure of the horse; and, more especially, will it be needful to obtain a general conception of the structure of its fore and hind limbs, and of its teeth. But I shall only touch upon those points which are absolutely essential to our inquiry.

Let us turn in the first place to the fore-limb. In most quadrupeds, as in ourselves, the fore-arm contains distinct bones called the radius and the ulna. The corresponding region in the Horse seem at first to possess but one bone. Careful observation, however, enables us to distinguish in this bone a part which clearly answers to the upper end of the ulna. This is closely united with the chief mass of the bone which represents the radius, and runs out into a slender shaft which may be traced for some distance downwards upon the back of the radius, and then in most cases thins out and vanishes. It takes still more trouble to make sure of what is nevertheless the fact, that a small part of the lower end of the bone of the horse's fore-arm, which is only distinct in a very young foal, is really the lower extremity of the ulna.

What is commonly called the knee of a horse is its wrist. The "cannon bone" answers to the middle bone of the five metacarpal bones, which support the palm of the hand in ourselves. The "pastern," "coronary," and "coffin" bones of veterinarians answer to the joints of our middle fingers, while the hoof is simply a greatly enlarged and thickened nail. But if what lies below the horse's "knee" thus corresponds to the middle finger in ourselves, what has become of the four other fingers or digits? We find in the places of the second and fourth digits only two slender splint-like bones, about two-thirds as long as the cannon bone, which gradually taper to their lower ends and bear no finger joints, or, as they are termed, phalanges. Sometimes, small bony or gristly nodules are to be found at the bases of these two metacarpal splints, and it is probable that these represent rudiments of the first and fifth toes. Thus, the part of the horse's skeleton, which corresponds with that of the human hand, contains one overgrown middle digit, and at least two imperfect lateral digits; and these answer, respectively, to the third, the second, and the fourth fingers in man.

Corresponding modifications are found in the hind limb. In ourselves, and in most quadrupeds, the leg contains two distinct bones, a large bone, the tibia, and a smaller and more slender bone, the fibula. But, in the horse, the fibula seems, at first, to be reduced to its upper end; a short slender bone united with the tibia, and ending in a point below, occupying its place. Examination of the lower end of a young foal's shin-bone, however, shows a distinct portion of osseous matter, which is the lower end of the fibula; so that the, apparently single, lower end of the shin-bone is really made up of the coalesced ends of the tibia and fibula, just as the, apparently single, lower end of the fore-arm bone is composed of the coalesced radius and ulna.

The heel of the horse is the part commonly known as the hock. The hinder cannon bone answers to the middle metatarsal bone of the human foot, the pastern, coronary, and coffin bones, to the middle toe bones; the hind hoof to the nail; as in the fore-foot. And, as in the fore-foot, there are merely two splints to represent the second and the fourth toes. Sometimes a rudiment of a fifth toe appears to be traceable.

The teeth of a horse are not less peculiar than its limbs. The living engine, like all others, must be well stoked if it is to do its work; and the horse, if it is to make good its wear and tear, and to exert the enormous amount of force required for its propulsion, must be well and rapidly fed. To this end, good cutting instruments and powerful and lasting crushers are needful. Accordingly, the twelve cutting teeth of a horse are close-set and concentrated in the fore part of its mouth, like so many adzes or chisels. The grinders or molars are large, and have an extremely complicated structure, being composed of a number of different substances of unequal hardness. The consequence of this is that they wear away at different rates; and, hence, the surface of each grinder is always as uneven as that of a good millstone.

I have said that the structure of the grinding teeth is very complicated, the harder and the softer parts being, as it were, interlaced with one another. The result of this is that, as the tooth wears, the crown presents a peculiar pattern, the nature of which is not very easily deciphered at first; but which it is important we should understand clearly. Each grinding tooth of the upper jaw has an *outer wall* so shaped that, on the worn crown, it exhibits the form of two crescents, one in front and one behind, with their concave sides turned outwards. From the inner side of the front crescent, a crescentic *front ridge* passes inwards and backwards, and its inner face enlarges into a strong longitudinal fold or *pillar*. From the front part of the hinder crescent, a *back ridge* takes a like direction, and also has its *pillar*.

The deep interspaces or *valleys* between these ridges and the outer wall are filled by bony substance, which is called *cement*, and coats the whole tooth.

The pattern of the worn face of each grinding tooth of the lower jaw is quite different. It appears to be formed of two crescent-shaped ridges, the convexities of which are turned outwards. The free extremity of each crescent has a *pillar*, and there is a large double *pillar* where the two crescents meet. The whole structure is, as it were, imbedded in cement, which fills up the valleys, as in the upper grinders.

If the grinding faces of an upper and of a lower molar of the same side are applied together, it will be seen that the apposed ridges are nowhere parallel, but that they frequently cross; and that thus, in the act of mastication, a hard surface in the one is constantly applied to a soft surface in the other, and *vice versâ*. They thus constitute a grinding apparatus of great efficiency, and one which is repaired as fast as it wears, owing to the long-continued growth of the teeth.

Some other peculiarities of the dentition of the horse must be noticed, as they bear upon what I shall have to say by and by. Thus the crowns of the cutting teeth have a peculiar deep pit, which gives rise to the well-known "mark" of the horse. There is a large space between the outer incisors and the front grinder. In this space the adult male horse presents, near the incisors on each side, above and below, a canine or "tush," which is commonly absent in mares. In a young horse, moreover, there is not unfrequently to be seen in front of the first grinder, a very small tooth, which soon falls out. If this small tooth be counted as one, it will be found that there are seven teeth behind the canine on each side; namely, the small tooth in question, and the six great grinders, among which, by an unusual peculiarity, the foremost tooth is rather larger than those which follow it.

I have now enumerated those characteristic structures of the horse which are of most importance for the purpose we have in view.

To any one who is acquainted with the morphology of vertebrated animals, they show that the horse deviates widely from the general structure of mammals; and that the horse type is, in many respects, an extreme modification of the general mammalian plan. The least modified mammals, in fact, have the radius and ulna, the tibia and fibula, distinct and separate. They have five distinct and complete digits on each foot, and no one of these digits is very much larger than the rest. Moreover, in the least modified mammals, the total number of the teeth is very generally forty-four, while in horses, the usual number is forty, and in the absence of the canines, it may be reduced to thirty-six; the incisor teeth are devoid of the fold seen in those of the horse: the grinders regularly diminish in size from the middle of the series to its front end; while their crowns are short, early attain their full length, and exhibit simple ridges or tubercles, in place of the complex foldings of the horse's grinders.

Hence the general principles of the hypothesis of evolution lead to the conclusion that the horse must have been derived from some quadruped which possessed five complete digits on each foot; which had the bones of the fore-arm and of the leg complete and separate; and which possessed forty-four teeth, among which the crowns of the incisors and grinders had a simple structure; while the latter gradually increased in size from before backwards, at any rate in the anterior part of the series, and had short crowns.

And if the horse has been thus evolved, and the remains of the different stages of its evolution have been preserved, they ought to present us with a series of forms in which the number of the digits becomes reduced; the bones of the fore-arm and leg gradually take on the equine condition; and the form and arrangement of the teeth successively approximate to those which obtain in existing horses.

Let us turn to the facts, and see how far they fulfil these requirements of the doctrine of evolution.

In Europe abundant remains of horses are found in the Quaternary and later Tertiary strata as far as the Pliocene formation. But these horses, which are so common in the cave-deposits and in the gravels of Europe, are in all essential respects like existing horses. And that is true of all the horses of the latter part of the Pliocene epoch. But, in deposits which belong to the earlier Pliocene and later Miocene epochs, and which occur in Britain, in France, in Germany, in Greece, in India, we find animals which are extremely like horses — which, in fact, are so similar to horses, that you may follow descriptions given in works upon the anatomy of the horse upon the skeletons of these animals — but which differ in some important particulars. For example, the structure of their fore and hind limbs is somewhat different. The bones which, in the horse, are represented by two splints, imperfect below, are as long as the middle metacarpal and metatarsal bones; and, attached to the extremity of each, is a digit with three joints of the same general character as those of the middle digit, only very much smaller. These small digits are so disposed that they could have had but very little functional importance, and they must have been rather of the nature of the dew-claws, such as are to be found in many ruminant animals. The *Hipparion*, as the extinct European three-toed horse is called, in fact, presents a foot similar to that of the American *Protohippus* (Fig. 9), except that, in the *Hipparion*, the smaller digits are situated farther back, and are of smaller proportional size, than in the *Protohippus*.

The ulna is slightly more distinct than in the horse; and the whole length of it, as a very slender shaft, intimately united with the radius, is completely traceable. The fibula appears to be in the same condition as in the horse. The teeth of the *Hipparion* are essentially similar to those of the horse, but the pattern of the grinders is in some respects a little more complex, and there is a depression on the face of the skull in front of the orbit, which is not seen in existing horses.

In the earlier Miocene, and perhaps the later Eocene deposits of some parts of Europe, another extinct animal has been discovered, which Cuvier, who first described some fragments of it, considered to be a *Palæotherium*. But as further discoveries threw new light upon its structure, it was recognised as a distinct genus, under the name of *Anchitherium*.

In its general characters, the skeleton of *Anchitherium* is very similar to that of the horse. In fact, Lartet and De Blainville called it *Palæotherium equinum* or *hippoides*; and De Christol, in 1847, said that it differed from *Hipparion* in little more than the characters of its teeth, and gave it the name of *Hipparitherium*. Each foot possesses three complete toes; while the lateral toes are much larger in proportion to the middle toe than in *Hipparion*, and doubtless rested on the ground in ordinary locomotion.

The ulna is complete and quite distinct from the radius, though firmly united with the latter. The fibula seems also to have been complete. Its lower end, though intimately united with that of the tibia, is clearly marked off from the latter bone.

There are forty-four teeth. The incisors have no strong pit. The canines seem to have been well developed in both sexes. The first of the seven grinders, which, as I have said, is frequently absent, and, when it does exist, is small in the horse, is a good-sized and permanent tooth, while the grinder which follows it is but little larger than the hinder ones. The crowns of the grinders are short, and though the fundamental pattern of the horse-tooth is discernible, the front and back ridges are less curved, the accessory pillars are wanting, and the valleys, much shallower, are not filled up with cement.

Seven years ago, when I happened to be looking critically into the bearing of palæontological facts upon the doctrine of evolution, it appeared to me that the *Anchitherium*, the *Hipparion*, and the modern horses, constitute a series in which the modifications of structure coincide with the order of chronological occurrence, in the manner in which they must coincide, if the modern horses really are the result of the gradual metamorphosis, in the course of the Tertiary epoch, of a less specialised ancestral form. And I found by correspondence with the late eminent French anatomist and palæontologist, M. Lartet, that he had arrived at the same conclusion from the same data.

That the *Anchitherium* type had become metamorphosed into the *Hipparion* type, and the latter into the *Equine* type, in the course of that period of time which is represented by the latter half of the Tertiary deposits, seemed to me to be the only explanation of the facts for which there was even a shadow of probability.[2]

And, hence, I have ever since held that these facts afford evidence of the occurrence of evolution, which, in the sense already defined, may be termed demonstrative.

All who have occupied themselves with the structure of *Anchitherium*, from Cuvier onwards, have acknowledged its many points of likeness to a well-known genus of extinct Eocene mammals, *Palæotherium*. Indeed, as we have seen, Cuvier regarded his remains of *Anchitherium* as those of a species of *Palæotherium*. Hence, in attempting to trace the pedigree of the horse beyond the Miocene epoch and the Anchitheroid form, I naturally sought among the various species of Palæotheroid animals for its nearest ally, and I was led to conclude that the *Palæotherium minus (Plagiolophus)* represented the next step more nearly than any form then known.

I think that this opinion was fully justifiable; but the progress of investigation has thrown an unexpected light on the question, and has brought us much nearer than could have been anticipated to a knowledge of the true series of the progenitors of the horse.

You are all aware that, when your country was first discovered by Europeans, there were no traces of the existence of the horse in any part of the American Continent. The accounts of the conquest of Mexico dwell upon the astonishment of the natives of that country when they first became acquainted with that astounding phenomenon — a man seated upon a horse. Nevertheless, the investigations of American geologists have proved that the remains of horses occur in the most superficial deposits of both North and South America, just as they do in Europe. Therefore, for some reason or other — no feasible suggestion on that subject, so far as I know, has been made — the horse must have died out on this continent at some period preceding the discovery of America. Of late years there has been discovered in your Western Territories that marvellous accumulation of deposits, admirably adapted for the preservation of organic remains, to which I referred the other evening, and which furnishes us with a consecutive series of records of the fauna of the older half of the Tertiary epoch, for which we have no parallel in Europe. They have yielded fossils in an excellent state of conservation and in unexampled number and variety. The researches of Leidy and others have shown that forms allied to the *Hipparion* and the *Anchitherium* are to be found among these remains. But it is only recently that the admirably conceived and most thoroughly and patiently worked-out investigations of Professor Marsh have given us a just idea of the vast fossil wealth, and of the scientific importance, of these deposits. I have had the advantage of glancing over the collections in Yale Museum; and I can truly say that, so far as my knowledge extends, there is no collection from any one region and series of strata comparable, for extent, or for the care with which the remains have been got together, or for their scientific importance, to the series of fossils which he has deposited there. This vast collection has yielded evidence bearing upon the question of the pedigree of the horse of the most striking character. It tends to show that we must look to America, rather than to Europe, for the original seat of the equine series; and that the archaic forms and successive modifications of the horse's ancestry are far better preserved here than in Europe.

Professor Marsh's kindness has enabled me to put before you a diagram, every figure in which is an actual representation of some specimen which is to be seen at Yale at this present time (Fig. 9).

The succession of forms which he has brought together carries us from the top to the bottom of the Tertiaries. Firstly, there is the true horse. Next we have the American Pliocene form of the horse (*Pliohippus*); in the conformation of its limbs it presents some very slight deviations from the ordinary horse, and the crowns of the grinding teeth are shorter. Then comes the *Protohippus*, which represents the European *Hipparion*, having one large digit and two small ones on each foot, and the general characters of the fore-arm and leg to which I have referred. But it is more valuable than the European *Hipparion* for the reason that it is devoid of some of the peculiarities of that form — peculiarities which tend to show that the European *Hipparion* is rather a member of a collateral branch, than a form in the direct line of succession. Next, in the backward order in time, is the *Miohippus*, which corresponds pretty nearly with the *Anchitherium* of Europe. It presents three complete toes — one large median and two smaller lateral ones; and there is a rudiment of that digit, which answers to the little finger of the human hand.

Fig. 9

The European record of the pedigree of the horse stops here; in the American Tertiaries, on the contrary, the series of ancestral equine forms is continued into the Eocene formations. An older Miocene form, termed *Mesohippus*, has three toes in front, with a large splint-like rudiment representing the little finger; and three toes behind. The radius and ulna, the tibia and the fibula, are distinct, and the short crowned molar teeth are anchitherioid in pattern.

But the most important discovery of all is the *Orohippus*, which comes from the Eocene formation, and is the oldest member of the equine series, as yet known. Here we find four complete toes on the front-limb, three toes on the hind-limb, a well-developed ulna, a well-developed fibula, and short-crowned grinders of simple pattern.

Thus, thanks to these important researches, it has become evident that, so far as our present knowledge extends, the history of the horse-type is exactly and precisely that which could have been predicted from a knowledge of the principles of evolution. And the knowledge we now possess justifies us completely in the anticipation, that when the still lower Eocene deposits, and those which belong to the Cretaceous epoch, have yielded up their remains of ancestral equine animals, we shall find, first, a form with four complete toes and a rudiment of the innermost or first digit in front, with, probably, a rudiment of the fifth digit in the hind foot;[3] while, in still older forms, the series of the digits will be more and more complete, until we come to the five-toed animals, in which, if the doctrine of evolution is well founded, the whole series must have taken its origin.

That is what I mean by demonstrative evidence of evolution. An inductive hypothesis is said to be demonstrated when the facts are shown to be in entire accordance with it. If that is not scientific proof, there are no merely inductive conclusions which can be said to be proved. And the doctrine of evolution, at the present time, rests upon exactly as secure a foundation as the Copernican theory of the motions of the heavenly bodies did at the time of its promulgation. Its logical basis is precisely of the same character — the coincidence of the observed facts with theoretical requirements.

The only way of escape, if it be a way of escape, from the conclusions which I have just indicated, is the supposition that all these different equine forms have been created separately at separate epochs of time; and, I repeat, that of such an hypothesis as this there neither is, nor can be, any scientific evidence; and, assuredly, so far as I know, there is none which is supported, or pretends to be supported, by evidence or authority of any other kind. I can but think that the time will come when such suggestions as these, such obvious attempts to escape the force of demonstration, will be put upon the same footing as the supposition made by some writers, who are, I believe, not completely extinct at present, that fossils are mere simulacra, are no indications of the former existence of the animals to which they seem to belong; but that they are either sports of Nature, or special creations, intended — as I heard suggested the other day — to test our faith.

In fact, the whole evidence is in favour of evolution, and there is none against it. And I say this, although perfectly well aware of the seeming difficulties which have been built up upon what appears to the uninformed to be a solid foundation. I meet constantly with the argument that the doctrine of evolution cannot be well founded, because it requires the lapse of a very vast period of time; the duration of life upon the earth, thus implied, is inconsistent with the conclusions arrived at by the astronomer and the physicist. I may venture to say that I am familiar with those conclusions, inasmuch as some years ago, when President of the Geological Society of London, I took the liberty of criticising them, and of showing in what respects, as it appeared to me, they lacked complete and thorough demonstration. But, putting that point aside, suppose that, as the astronomers, or some of them, and some physical philosophers, tell us, it is impossible that life could have endured upon the earth for as long a period as is required by the doctrine of evolution — supposing that to be proved — I desire to be informed, what is the foundation for the statement that evolution does require so great a time? The biologist knows nothing whatever of the amount of time which may be required for the process of evolution. It is a matter of fact that the equine forms which I have described to you occur, in the order stated, in the Tertiary formations. But I have not the slightest means of guessing whether it took a million of years, or ten millions, or a hundred millions, or a thousand millions of years, to give rise to that series of changes. A biologist has no means of arriving at any conclusion as to the amount of time which may be needed for a certain quantity of organic change. He takes his time from the geologist. The geologist, considering the rate at which deposits are formed and the rate at which denudation goes on upon the surface of the earth, arrives at more or less justifiable conclusions as to the time which is required for the deposit of a certain thickness of rocks; and if he tells me that the Tertiary formations required 500,000,000 years for their deposit, I suppose he has good ground for what he says, and I take that as a measure of the duration of the evolution of the horse from the *Orohippus* up to its present condition. And, if he is right, undoubtedly evolution is a very slow process, and requires a great deal of time. But suppose, now, that an astronomer or a physicist — for instance, my friend Sir William Thomson — tells me that my geological authority is quite wrong; and that he has weighty evidence to show that life could not possibly have existed upon the surface of the earth 500,000,000 years ago, because the earth would have then been too hot to allow of life, my reply is: "That is not my affair; settle that with the geologist, and when you have come to an agreement among yourselves I will adopt your conclusion." We take our time from the geologists and physicists; and it is monstrous that, having taken our time from the physical philosopher's clock, the physical philosopher should turn round upon us, and say we are too fast or too slow. What we desire to know is, is it a fact that evolution took place? As to the amount of time which evolution may have occupied, we are in the hands of the physicist and the astronomer, whose business it is to deal with those questions.

I have now, ladies and gentlemen, arrived at the conclusion of the task which I set before myself when I undertook to deliver these lectures. My purpose has been, not to enable those among you who have paid no attention to these subjects before, to leave this room in a condition to decide upon the validity or the invalidity of the hypothesis of evolution; but I have desired to put before you the principles upon which all hypotheses respecting the history of Nature must be judged; and furthermore, to make apparent the nature of the evidence and the amount of cogency which is to be expected and may be obtained from it. To this end, I have not hesitated to regard you as genuine students and persons desirous of knowing the truth. I have not shrunk from taking you through long discussions, that I fear may have sometimes tried your patience; and I have inflicted upon you details which were indispensable, but which may well have been wearisome. But I shall rejoice—I shall consider that I have done you the greatest service, which it was in my power to do—if I have thus convinced you that the great question which we have been discussing is not one to be dealt with by rhetorical flourishes, or by loose and superficial talk; but that it requires the keen attention of the trained intellect and the patience of the accurate observer.

When I commenced this series of lectures, I did not think it necessary to preface them with a prologue, such as might be expected from a stranger and a foreigner; for during my brief stay in your country, I have found it very hard to believe that a stranger could be possessed of so many friends, and almost harder that a foreigner could express himself in your language in such a way as to be, to all appearance, so readily intelligible. So far as I can judge, that most intelligent, and, perhaps, I may add, most singularly active and enterprising body, your press reporters, do not seem to have been deterred by my accent from giving the fullest account of everything that I happen to have said.

But the vessel in which I take my departure to-morrow morning is even now ready to slip her moorings; I awake from my delusion that I am other than a stranger and a foreigner. I am ready to go back to my place and country; but, before doing so, let me, by way of epilogue, tender to you my most hearty thanks for the kind and cordial reception which you have accorded to me; and let me thank you still more for that which is the greatest compliment which can be afforded to any person in my position— the continuous and undisturbed attention which you have bestowed upon the long argument which I have had the honour to lay before you.

[1] The absence of any keel on the breast-bone and some other osteological peculiarities, observed by Professor Marsh, however, suggest that *Hesperornis* may be a modification of a less specialised group of birds than that to which these existing aquatic birds belong.

[2] I use the word "type" because it is highly probable that many forms of *Anchitherium*-like and *Hipparion*-like animals existed in the Miocene and Pliocene epochs, just as many species of the horse tribe exist now; and it is highly improbable that the particular species of *Anchitherium* or *Hipparion*, which happen to have been discovered, should be precisely those which have formed part of the direct line of the horse's pedigree.

[3] Since this lecture was delivered, Professor Marsh has discovered a new genus of equine mammals (*Eohippus*) from the lowest Eocene deposits of the West, which corresponds very nearly to this description. — *American Journal of Science*, November, 1876.

BALTIMORE

ADDRESS ON UNIVERSITY EDUCATION[1]

The actual work of the University founded in this city by the well-considered munificence of Johns Hopkins commences to-morrow, and among the many marks of confidence and good-will which have been bestowed upon me in the United States, there is none which I value more highly than that conferred by the authorities of the University when they invited me to deliver an address on such an occasion.

For the event which has brought us together is, in many respects, unique. A vast property is handed over to an administrative body, hampered by no conditions save these;—That the principal shall not be employed in building: that the funds shall be appropriated, in equal proportions, to the promotion of natural knowledge and to the alleviation of the bodily sufferings of mankind; and, finally, that neither political nor ecclesiastical sectarianism shall be permitted to disturb the impartial distribution of the testator's benefactions.

In my experience of life a truth which sounds very much like a paradox has often asserted itself; namely, that a man's worst difficulties begin when he is able to do as he likes. So long as a man is struggling with obstacles he has an excuse for failure or shortcoming; but when fortune removes them all and gives him the power of doing as he thinks best, then comes the time of trial. There is but one right, and the possibilities of wrong are infinite. I doubt not that the trustees of the Johns Hopkins University felt the full force of this truth when they entered on the administration of their trust a year and a half ago; and I can but admire the activity and resolution which have enabled them, aided by the able president whom they have selected, to lay down the great outlines of their plan, and carry it thus far into execution. It is impossible to study that plan without perceiving that great care, forethought, and sagacity, have been bestowed upon it, and that it demands the most respectful consideration. I have been endeavouring to ascertain how far the principles which underlie it are in accordance with those which have been established in my own mind by much and long-continued thought upon educational questions. Permit me to place before you the result of my reflections.

Under one aspect a university is a particular kind of educational institution, and the views which we may take of the proper nature of a university are corollaries from those which we hold respecting education in general. I think it must be admitted that the school should prepare for the university, and that the university should crown the edifice, the foundations of which are laid in the school. University education should not be something distinct from elementary education, but should be the natural outgrowth and development of the latter. Now I have a very clear conviction as to what elementary education ought to be; what it really may be, when properly organised; and what I think it will be, before many years have passed over our heads, in England and in America. Such education should enable an average boy of fifteen or sixteen to read and write his own language with ease and accuracy, and with a sense of literary excellence derived from the study of our classic writers: to have a general acquaintance with the history of his own country and with the great laws of social existence; to have acquired the rudiments of the physical and psychological sciences, and a fair knowledge of elementary arithmetic and geometry. He should have obtained an acquaintance with logic rather by example than by precept; while the acquirement of the elements of music and drawing should have been pleasure rather than work.

It may sound strange to many ears if I venture to maintain the proposition that a young person, educated thus far, has had a liberal, though perhaps not a full, education. But it seems to me that such training as that to which I have referred may be termed liberal, in both the senses in which that word is employed, with perfect accuracy. In the first place, it is liberal in breadth. It extends over the whole ground of things to be known and of faculties to be trained, and it gives equal importance to the two great sides of human activity—art and science. In the second place, it is liberal in the sense of being an education fitted for free men; for men to whom every career is open, and from whom their country may demand that they should be fitted to perform the duties of any career. I cannot too strongly impress upon you the fact that, with such a primary education as this, and with no more than is to be obtained by building strictly upon its lines, a man of ability may become a great writer or speaker, a statesman, a lawyer, a man of science, painter, sculptor, architect, or musician. That even development of all a man's faculties, which is what properly constitutes culture, may be effected by such an education, while it opens the way for the indefinite strengthening of any special capabilities with which he may be gifted.

In a country like this, where most men have to carve out their own fortunes and devote themselves early to the practical affairs of life, comparatively few can hope to pursue their studies up to, still less beyond, the age of manhood. But it is of vital importance to the welfare of the community that those who are relieved from the need of making a livelihood, and still more, those who are stirred by the divine impulses of intellectual thirst or artistic genius, should be enabled to devote themselves to the higher service of their kind, as centres of intelligence, interpreters of nature, or creators of new forms of beauty. And it is the function of a university to furnish such men with the means of becoming that which it is their privilege and duty to be. To this end the university need cover no ground foreign to that occupied by the elementary school. Indeed it cannot; for the elementary instruction which I have referred to embraces all the kinds of real knowledge and mental activity possible to man. The university can add no new departments of knowledge, can offer no new fields of mental activity; but what it can do is to intensify and specialise the instruction in each department. Thus literature and philology, represented in the elementary school by English alone, in the university will extend over the ancient and modern languages. History, which, like charity, best begins at home, but, like charity, should not end there, will ramify into anthropology, archæology, political history, and geography, with the history of the growth of the human mind and of its products in the shape of philosophy, science, and art. And the university will present to the student libraries, museums of antiquities, collections of coins, and the like, which will efficiently subserve these studies. Instruction in the elements of social economy, a most essential, but hitherto sadly-neglected part of elementary education, will develop in the university into political economy, sociology, and law. Physical science will have its great divisions of physical geography, with geology and astronomy; physics; chemistry and biology; represented not merely by professors and their lectures, but by laboratories, in which the students, under guidance of demonstrators, will work out facts for themselves and come into that direct contact with reality which constitutes the fundamental distinction of scientific education. Mathematics will soar into its highest regions; while the high peaks of philosophy may be scaled by those whose aptitude for abstract thought has been awakened by elementary logic. Finally, schools of pictorial and plastic art, of architecture, and of music, will offer a thorough discipline in the principles and practice of art to those in whom lies nascent the rare faculty of æsthetic representation, or the still rarer powers of creative genius.

The primary school and the university are the alpha and omega of education. Whether institutions intermediate between these (so-called secondary schools) should exist, appears to me to be a question of practical convenience. If such schools are established, the important thing is that they should be true intermediaries between the primary school and the university, keeping on the wide track of general culture, and not sacrificing one branch of knowledge for another.

Such appear to me to be the broad outlines of the relations which the university, regarded as a place of education, ought to bear to the school, but a number of points of detail require some consideration, however briefly and imperfectly I can deal with them. In the first place, there is the important question of the limitations which should be fixed to the entrance into the university; or, what qualifications should be required of those who propose to take advantage of the higher training offered by the university. On the one hand, it is obviously desirable that the time and opportunities of the university should not be wasted in conferring such elementary instruction as can be obtained elsewhere; while, on the other hand, it is no less desirable that the higher instruction of the university should be made accessible to every one who can take advantage of it, although he may not have been able to go through any very extended course of education. My own feeling is distinctly against any absolute and defined preliminary examination, the passing of which shall be an essential condition of admission to the university. I would admit to the university any one who could be reasonably expected to profit by the instruction offered to him; and I should be inclined, on the whole, to test the fitness of the student, not by examination before he enters the university, but at the end of his first term of study. If, on examination in the branches of knowledge to which he has devoted himself, he show himself deficient in industry or in capacity, it will be best for the university and best for himself, to prevent him from pursuing a vocation for which he is obviously unfit. And I hardly know of any other method than this by which his fitness or unfitness can be safely ascertained, though no doubt a good deal may be done, not by formal cut and dried examination, but by judicious questioning, at the outset of his career.

Another very important and difficult practical question is, whether a definite course of study shall be laid down for those who enter the university; whether a curriculum shall be prescribed; or whether the student shall be allowed to range at will among the subjects which are open to him. And this question is inseparably connected with another, namely, the conferring of degrees. It is obviously impossible that any student should pass through the whole of the series of courses of instruction offered by a university. If a degree is to be conferred as a mark of proficiency in knowledge, it must be given on the ground that the candidate is proficient in a certain fraction of those studies; and then will arise the necessity of insuring an equivalency of degrees, so that the course by which a degree is obtained shall mark approximately an equal amount of labour and of acquirements, in all cases. But this equivalency can hardly be secured in any other way than by prescribing a series of definite lines of study. This is a matter which will require grave consideration. The important points to bear in mind, I think, are that there should not be too many subjects in the curriculum, and that the aim should be the attainment of thorough and sound knowledge of each.

One half of the Johns Hopkins bequest is devoted to the establishment of a hospital, and it was the desire of the testator that the university and the hospital should co-operate in the promotion of medical education. The trustees will unquestionably take the best advice that is to be had as to the construction and administration of the hospital. In respect to the former point, they will doubtless remember that a hospital may be so arranged as to kill more than it cures; and, in regard to the latter, that a hospital may spread the spirit of pauperism among the well-to-do, as well as relieve the sufferings of the destitute. It is not for me to speak on these topics — rather let me confine myself to the one matter on which my experience as a student of medicine, and an examiner of long standing, who has taken a great interest in the subject of medical education, may entitle me to a hearing. I mean the nature of medical education itself, and the co-operation of the university in its promotion.

What is the object of medical education? It is to enable the practitioner, on the one hand, to prevent disease by his knowledge of hygiene; on the other hand, to divine its nature, and to alleviate or cure it, by his knowledge of pathology, therapeutics, and practical medicine. That is his business in life, and if he has not a thorough and practical knowledge of the conditions of health, of the causes which tend to the establishment of disease, of the meaning of symptoms, and of the uses of medicines and operative appliances, he is incompetent, even if he were the best anatomist, or physiologist, or chemist, that ever took a gold medal or won a prize certificate. This is one great truth respecting medical education. Another is, that all practice in medicine is based upon theory of some sort or other; and therefore, that it is desirable to have such theory in the closest possible accordance with fact. The veriest empiric who gives a drug in one case because he has seen it do good in another of apparently the same sort, acts upon the theory that similarity of superficial symptoms means similarity of lesions; which, by the way, is perhaps as wild an hypothesis as could be invented. To understand the nature of disease we must understand health, and the understanding of the healthy body means the having a knowledge of its structure and of the way in which its manifold actions are performed, which is what is technically termed human anatomy and human physiology.

The physiologist again must needs possess an acquaintance with physics and chemistry, inasmuch as physiology is, to a great extent, applied physics and chemistry. For ordinary purposes a limited amount of such knowledge is all that is needful; but for the pursuit of the higher branches of physiology no knowledge of these branches of science can be too extensive, or too profound. Again, what we call therapeutics, which has to do with the action of drugs and medicines on the living organism, is, strictly speaking, a branch of experimental physiology, and is daily receiving a greater and greater experimental development.

The third great fact which is to be taken into consideration in dealing with medical education, is that the practical necessities of life do not, as a rule, allow aspirants to medical practice to give more than three, or it may be four years to their studies. Let us put it at four years, and then reflect that, in the course of this time, a young man fresh from school has to acquaint himself with medicine, surgery, obstetrics, therapeutics, pathology, hygiene, as well as with the anatomy and the physiology of the human body; and that his knowledge should be of such a character that it can be relied upon in any emergency, and always ready for practical application. Consider, in addition, that the medical practitioner may be called upon, at any moment, to give evidence in a court of justice in a criminal case; and that it is therefore well that he should know something of the laws of evidence, and of what we call medical jurisprudence. On a medical certificate, a man may be taken from his home and from his business and confined in a lunatic asylum; surely, therefore, it is desirable that the medical practitioner should have some rational and clear conceptions as to the nature and symptoms of mental disease. Bearing in mind all these requirements of medical education, you will admit that the burden on the young aspirant for the medical profession is somewhat of the heaviest, and that it needs some care to prevent his intellectual back from being broken.

Those who are acquainted with the existing systems of medical education will observe that, long as is the catalogue of studies which I have enumerated, I have omitted to mention several that enter into the usual medical curriculum of the present day. I have said not a word about zoology, comparative anatomy, botany, or materia medica. Assuredly this is from no light estimate of the value or importance of such studies in themselves. It may be taken for granted that I should be the last person in the world to object to the teaching of zoology, or comparative anatomy, in themselves; but I have the strongest feeling that, considering the number and the gravity of those studies through which a medical man must pass, if he is to be competent to discharge the serious duties which devolve upon him, subjects which lie so remote as these do from his practical pursuits should be rigorously excluded. The young man, who has enough to do in order to acquire such familiarity with the structure of the human body as will enable him to perform the operations of surgery, ought not, in my judgment, to be occupied with investigations into the anatomy of crabs and starfishes. Undoubtedly the doctor should know the common poisonous plants of his own country when he sees them; but that knowledge may be obtained by a few hours devoted to the examination of specimens of such plants, and the desirableness of such knowledge is no justification, to my mind, for spending three months over the study of systematic botany. Again, materia medica, so far as it is a knowledge of drugs, is the business of the druggist. In all other callings the necessity of the division of labour is fully recognised, and it is absurd to require of the medical man that he should not avail himself of the special knowledge of those whose business it is to deal in the drugs which he uses. It is all very well that the physician should know that castor oil comes from a plant, and castoreum from an animal, and how they are to be prepared; but for all the practical purposes of his profession that knowledge is not of one whit more value, has no more relevancy, than the knowledge of how the steel of his scalpel is made.

All knowledge is good. It is impossible to say that any fragment of knowledge, however insignificant or remote from one's ordinary pursuits, may not some day be turned to account. But in medical education, above all things, it is to be recollected that, in order to know a little well, one must be content to be ignorant of a great deal.

Let it not be supposed that I am proposing to narrow medical education, or, as the cry is, to lower the standard of the profession. Depend upon it there is only one way of really ennobling any calling, and that is to make those who pursue it real masters of their craft, men who can truly do that which they profess to be able to do, and which they are credited with being able to do by the public. And there is no position so ignoble as that of the so-called "liberally-educated practitioner," who, as Talleyrand said of his physician, "Knows everything, even a little physic;" who may be able to read Galen in the original; who knows all the plants, from the cedar of Lebanon to the hyssop upon the wall; but who finds himself, with the issues of life and death in his hands, ignorant, blundering, and bewildered, because of his ignorance of the essential and fundamental truths upon which practice must be based. Moreover, I venture to say, that any man who has seriously studied all the essential branches of medical knowledge; who has the needful acquaintance with the elements of physical science; who has been brought by medical jurisprudence into contact with law; whose study of insanity has taken him into the fields of psychology; has *ipso facto* received a liberal education.

Having lightened the medical curriculum by culling out of it everything which is unessential, we may next consider whether something may not be done to aid the medical student toward the acquirement of real knowledge by modifying the system of examination. In England, within my recollection, it was the practice to require of the medical student attendance on lectures upon the most diverse topics during three years; so that it often happened that he would have to listen, in the course of a day, to four or five lectures upon totally different subjects, in addition to the hours given to dissection and to hospital practice: and he was required to keep all the knowledge he could pick up, in this distracting fashion, at examination point, until, at the end of three years, he was set down to a table and questioned pell-mell upon all the different matters with which he had been striving to make acquaintance. A worse system and one more calculated to obstruct the acquisition of sound knowledge and to give full play to the "crammer" and the "grinder" could hardly have been devised by human ingenuity. Of late years great reforms have taken place. Examinations have been divided· so as to diminish the number of subjects among which the attention has to be distributed. Practical examination has been largely introduced; but there still remains, even under the present system, too much of the old evil inseparable from the contemporaneous pursuit of a multiplicity of diverse studies.

Proposals have recently been made to get rid of general examinations altogether, to permit the student to be examined in each subject at the end of his attendance on the class; and then, in case of the result being satisfactory, to allow him to have done with it; and I may say that this method has been pursued for many years in the Royal School of Mines in London, and has been found to work very well. It allows the student to concentrate his mind upon what he is about for the time being, and then to dismiss it. Those who are occupied in intellectual work, will, I think, agree with me that it is important, not so much to know a thing, as to have known it, and known it thoroughly. If you have once known a thing in this way it is easy to renew your knowledge when you have forgotten it; and when you begin to take the subject up again, it slides back upon the familiar grooves with great facility.

Lastly comes the question as to how the university may co-operate in advancing medical education. A medical school is strictly a technical school — a school in which a practical profession is taught — while a university ought to be a place in which knowledge is obtained without direct reference to professional purposes. It is clear, therefore, that a university and its antecedent, the school, may best co-operate with the medical school by making due provision for the study of those branches of knowledge which lie at the foundation of medicine.

At present, young men come to the medical schools without a conception of even the elements of physical science; they learn, for the first time, that there are such sciences as physics, chemistry, and physiology, and are introduced to anatomy as a new thing. It may be safely said that, with a large proportion of medical students, much of the first session is wasted in learning how to learn — in familiarising themselves with utterly strange conceptions, and in awakening their dormant and wholly untrained powers of observation and of manipulation. It is difficult to overestimate the magnitude of the obstacles which are thrown in the way of scientific training by the existing system of school education. Not only are men trained in mere book-work, ignorant of what observation means, but the habit of learning from books alone begets a disgust of observation. The book-learned student will rather trust to what he sees in a book than to the witness of his own eyes.

There is not the least reason why this should be so, and, in fact, when elementary education becomes that which I have assumed it ought to be, this state of things will no longer exist. There is not the slightest difficulty in giving sound elementary instruction in physics, in chemistry, and in the elements of human physiology, in ordinary schools. In other words, there is no reason why the student should not come to the medical school, provided with as much knowledge of these several sciences as he ordinarily picks up, in the course of his first year of attendance, at the medical school.

I am not saying this without full practical justification for the statement. For the last eighteen years we have had in England a system of elementary science teaching carried out under the auspices of the Science and Art Department, by which elementary scientific instruction is made readily accessible to the scholars of all the elementary schools in the country. Commencing with small beginnings, carefully developed and improved, that system now brings up for examination as many as seven thousand scholars in the subject of human physiology alone. I can say that, out of that number, a large proportion have acquired a fair amount of substantial knowledge; and that no inconsiderable percentage show as good an acquaintance with human physiology as used to be exhibited by the average candidates for medical degrees in the University of London, when I was first an examiner there twenty years ago; and quite as much knowledge as is possessed by the ordinary student of medicine at the present day. I am justified, therefore, in looking forward to the time when the student who proposes to devote himself to medicine will come, not absolutely raw and inexperienced as he is at present, but in a certain state of preparation for further study; and I look to the university to help him still further forward in that stage of preparation, through the organisation of its biological department. Here the student will find means of acquainting himself with the phenomena of life in their broadest acceptation. He will study not botany and zoology, which, as I have said, would take him too far away from his ultimate goal; but, by duly arranged instruction, combined with work in the laboratory upon the leading types of animal and vegetable life, he will lay a broad, and at the same time solid, foundation of biological knowledge; he will come to his medical studies with a comprehension of the great truths of morphology and of physiology, with his hands trained to dissect and his eyes taught to see. I have no hesitation in saying that such preparation is worth a full year added on to the medical curriculum. In other words, it will set free that much time for attention to those studies which bear directly upon the student's most grave and serious duties as a medical practitioner.

Up to this point I have considered only the teaching aspect of your great foundation, that function of the university in virtue of which it plays the part of a reservoir of ascertained truth, so far as our symbols can ever interpret nature. All can learn; all can drink of this lake. It is given to few to add to the store of knowledge, to strike new springs of thought, or to shape new forms of beauty. But so sure as it is that men live not by bread, but by ideas, so sure is it that the future of the world lies in the hands of those who are able to carry the interpretation of nature a step further than their predecessors; so certain is it that the highest function of a university is to seek out those men, cherish them, and give their ability to serve their kind full play.

I rejoice to observe that the encouragement of research occupies so prominent a place in your official documents, and in the wise and liberal inaugural address of your president. This subject of the encouragement, or, as it is sometimes called, the endowment of research, has of late years greatly exercised the minds of men in England. It was one of the main topics of discussion by the members of the Royal Commission of whom I was one, and who not long since issued their report, after five years' labour. Many seem to think that this question is mainly one of money; that you can go into the market and buy research, and that supply will follow demand, as in the ordinary course of commerce. This view does not commend itself to my mind. I know of no more difficult practical problem than the discovery of a method of encouraging and supporting the original investigator without opening the door to nepotism and jobbery. My own conviction is admirably summed up in the passage of your president's address, "that the best investigators are usually those who have also the responsibilities of instruction, gaining thus the incitement of colleagues, the encouragement of pupils, and the observation of the public."

At the commencement of this address I ventured to assume that I might, if I thought fit, criticise the arrangements which have been made by the board of trustees, but I confess that I have little to do but to applaud them. Most wise and sagacious seems to me the determination not to build for the present. It has been my fate to see great educational funds fossilise into mere bricks and mortar, in the petrifying springs of architecture, with nothing left to work the institution they were intended to support. A great warrior is said to have made a desert and called it peace. Administrators of educational funds have sometimes made a palace and called it a university. If I may venture to give advice in a matter which lies out of my proper competency, I would say that whenever you do build, get an honest bricklayer, and make him build you just such rooms as you really want, leaving ample space for expansion. And a century hence, when the Baltimore and Ohio shares are at one thousand premium, and you have endowed all the professors you need, and built all the laboratories that are wanted, and have the best museum and the finest library that can be imagined; then, if you have a few hundred thousand dollars you don't know what to do with, send for an architect and tell him to put up a façade. If American is similar to English experience, any other course will probably lead you into having some stately structure, good for your architect's fame, but not in the least what you want.

It appears to me that what I have ventured to lay down as the principles which should govern the relations of a university to education in general, are entirely in accordance with the measures you have adopted. You have set no restrictions upon access to the instruction you propose to give; you have provided that such instruction, either as given by the university or by associated institutions, should cover the field of human intellectual activity. You have recognised the importance of encouraging research. You propose to provide means by which young men, who may be full of zeal for a literary or for a scientific career, but who also may have mistaken aspiration for inspiration, may bring their capacities to a test, and give their powers a fair trial. If such a one fail, his endowment terminates, and there is no harm done. If he succeed, you may give power of flight to the genius of a Davy or a Faraday, a Carlyle or a Locke, whose influence on the future of his fellow-men shall be absolutely incalculable.

You have enunciated the principle that "the glory of the university should rest upon the character of the teachers and scholars, and not upon their numbers or buildings constructed for their use." And I look upon it as an essential and most important feature of your plan that the income of the professors and teachers shall be independent of the number of students whom they can attract. In this way you provide against the danger, patent elsewhere, of finding attempts at improvement obstructed by vested interests; and, in the department of medical education especially, you are free of the temptation to set loose upon the world men utterly incompetent to perform the serious and responsible duties of their profession.

It is a delicate matter for a stranger to the practical working of your institutions, like myself, to pretend to give an opinion as to the organisation of your governing power. I can conceive nothing better than that it should remain as it is, if you can secure a succession of wise, liberal, honest, and conscientious men to fill the vacancies that occur among you. I do not greatly believe in the efficacy of any kind of machinery for securing such a result; but I would venture to suggest that the exclusive adoption of the method of co-optation for filling the vacancies which must occur in your body, appears to me to be somewhat like a tempting of Providence. Doubtless there are grave practical objections to the appointment of persons outside of your body and not directly interested in the welfare of the university; but might it not be well if there were an understanding that your academic staff should be officially represented on the board, perhaps even the heads of one or two independent learned bodies, so that academic opinion and the views of the outside world might have a certain influence in that most important matter, the appointment of your professors? I throw out these suggestions, as I have said, in ignorance of the practical difficulties that may lie in the way of carrying them into effect, on the general ground that personal and local influences are very subtle, and often unconscious, while the future greatness and efficiency of the noble institution which now commences its work must largely depend upon its freedom from them.

I constantly hear Americans speak of the charm which our old mother country has for them, of the delight with which they wander through the streets of ancient towns, or climb the battlements of mediæval strongholds, the names of which are indissolubly associated with the great epochs of that noble literature which is our common inheritance; or with the blood-stained steps of that secular progress, by which the descendants of the savage Britons and of the wild pirates of the North Sea have become converted into warriors of order and champions of peaceful freedom, exhausting what still remains of the old Berserk spirit in subduing nature, and turning the wilderness into a garden. But anticipation has no less charm than retrospect, and to an Englishman landing upon your shores for the first time, travelling for hundreds of miles through strings of great and well-ordered cities, seeing your enormous actual, and almost infinite potential, wealth in all commodities, and in the energy and ability which turn wealth to account, there is something sublime in the vista of the future. Do not suppose that I am pandering to what is commonly understood by national pride. I cannot say that I am in the slightest degree impressed by your bigness, or your material resources, as such. Size is not grandeur, and territory does not make a nation. The great issue, about which hangs a true sublimity, and the terror of overhanging fate, is what are you going to do with all these things? What is to be the end to which these are to be the means? You are making a novel experiment in politics on the greatest scale which the world has yet seen. Forty millions at your first centenary, it is reasonably to be expected that, at the second, these states will be occupied by two hundred millions of English-speaking people, spread over an area as large as that of Europe, and with climates and interests as diverse as those of Spain and Scandinavia, England and Russia. You and your descendants have to ascertain whether this great mass will hold together under the forms of a republic, and the despotic reality of universal suffrage; whether state rights will hold out against centralisation, without separation; whether centralisation will get the better, without actual or disguised monarchy; whether shifting corruption is better than a permanent bureaucracy; and as population thickens in your great cities, and the pressure of want is felt, the gaunt spectre of pauperism will stalk among you, and communism and socialism will claim to be heard. Truly America has a great future before her; great in toil, in care, and in responsibility; great in true glory if she be guided in wisdom and righteousness; great in shame if she fail. I cannot understand why other nations should envy you, or be blind to the fact that it is for the highest interest of mankind that you should succeed; but the one condition of success, your sole safeguard, is the moral worth and intellectual clearness of the individual citizen. Education cannot give these, but it may cherish them and bring them to the front in whatever station of society they are to be found; and the universities ought to be, and may be, the fortresses of the higher life of the nation.

May the university which commences its practical activity to-morrow abundantly fulfil its high purpose; may its renown as a seat of true learning, a centre of free inquiry, a focus of intellectual light, increase year by year, until men wander hither from all parts of the earth, as of old they sought Bologna, or Paris, or Oxford.

And it is pleasant to me to fancy that, among the English students who are drawn to you at that time, there may linger a dim tradition that a countryman of theirs was permitted to address you as he has done to-day, and to feel as if your hopes were his hopes and your success his joy.

[1] Delivered at the formal opening of the Johns
Hopkins University at Baltimore, U.S., September 12.
The total amount bequeathed by Johns Hopkins is more
than 7,000,000 dollars. The sum of 3,500,000 dollars is
appropriated to a university, a like sum to a hospital, and
the rest to local institutions of education and charity.

LONDON

LECTURE ON THE STUDY OF BIOLOGY

It is my duty to-night to speak about the study of Biology, and while it may be that there are many of my audience who are quite familiar with that study, yet as a lecturer of some standing, it would, I know by experience, be very bad policy on my part to suppose such to be extensively the case. On the contrary, I must imagine that there are many of you who would like to know what Biology is; that there are others who have that amount of information, but would nevertheless gladly hear why it should be worth their while to study Biology; and yet others, again, to whom these two points are clear, but who desire to learn how they had best study it, and, finally, when they had best study it.

I shall, therefore, address myself to the endeavour to give you some answer to these four questions—what Biology is; why it should be studied; how it should be studied; and when it should be studied.

In the first place, in respect to what Biology is, there are, I believe, some persons who imagine that the term "Biology" is simply a new-fangled denomination, a neologism in short, for what used to be known under the title of "Natural History;" but I shall try to show you, on the contrary, that the word is the expression of the growth of science during the last 200 years, and came into existence half a century ago.

At the revival of learning, knowledge was divided into two kinds—the knowledge of nature and the knowledge of man; for it was the current idea then (and a great deal of that ancient conception still remains) that there was a sort of essential antithesis, not to say antagonism, between nature and man; and that the two had not very much to do with one another, except that the one was oftentimes exceedingly troublesome to the other. Though it is one of the salient merits of our great philosophers of the seventeenth century, that they recognised but one scientific method, applicable alike to man and to nature, we find this notion of the existence of a broad distinction between nature and man in the writings both of Bacon and of Hobbes of Malmesbury; and I have brought with me that famous work which is now so little known, greatly as it deserves to be studied, "The Leviathan," in order that I may put to you in the wonderfully terse and clear language of Thomas Hobbes, what was his view of the matter. He says:—

> "The register of knowledge of fact is called history.
> Whereof there be two sorts, one called natural history;
> which is the history of such facts or effects of nature
> as have no dependence on man's will; such as are the
> histories of metals, plants, animals, regions, and the
> like. The other is civil history; which is the history of
> the voluntary actions of men in commonwealths."

So that all history of fact was divided into these two great groups of natural and of civil history. The Royal Society was in course of foundation about the time that Hobbes was writing this book, which was published in 1651; and that Society was termed a "Society for the Improvement of Natural Knowledge," which was then nearly the same thing as a "Society for the Improvement of Natural History." As time went on, and the various branches of human knowledge became more distinctly developed and separated from one another, it was found that some were much more susceptible of precise mathematical treatment than others. The publication of the "Principia" of Newton, which probably gave a greater stimulus to physical science than any work ever published before, or which is likely to be published hereafter, showed that precise mathematical methods were applicable to those branches of science such as astronomy, and what we now call physics, which occupy a very large portion of the domain of what the older writers understood by natural history. And inasmuch as the partly deductive and partly experimental methods of treatment to which Newton and others subjected these branches of human knowledge, showed that the phenomena of nature which belonged to them were susceptible of explanation, and thereby came within the reach of what was called "philosophy" in those days; so much of this kind of knowledge as was not included under astronomy came to be spoken of as "natural philosophy"—a term which Bacon had employed in a much wider sense. Time went on, and yet other branches of science developed themselves. Chemistry took a definite shape; and since all these sciences, such as astronomy, natural philosophy, and chemistry, were susceptible either of mathematical treatment or of experimental treatment, or of both, a broad distinction was drawn between the experimental branches of what had previously been called natural history and the observational branches—those in which experiment was (or appeared to be) of doubtful use, and where, at that time, mathematical methods were inapplicable. Under these circumstances the old name of "Natural History" stuck by the residuum, by those phenomena which were not, at that time, susceptible of mathematical or experimental treatment; that is to say, those phenomena of nature which come now under the general heads of physical geography, geology, mineralogy, the history of plants, and the history of animals. It was in this sense that the term was understood by the great writers of the middle of the last century — Buffon and Linnæus — by Buffon in his great work, the "Histoire Naturelle Générale," and by Linnæus in his splendid achievement, the "Systema Naturæ." The subjects they deal with are spoken of as "Natural History," and they called themselves and were called "Naturalists." But you will observe that this was not the original meaning of these terms; but that they had, by this time, acquired a signification widely different from that which they possessed primitively.

The sense in which "Natural History" was used at the time I am now speaking of has, to a certain extent, endured to the present day. There are now in existence in some of our northern universities, chairs of "Civil and Natural History," in which "Natural History" is used to indicate exactly what Hobbes and Bacon meant by that term. The unhappy incumbent of the chair of Natural History is, or was, supposed to cover the whole ground of geology, mineralogy, and zoology, perhaps even botany, in his lectures.

But as science made the marvellous progress which it did make at the latter end of the last and the beginning of the present century, thinking men began to discern that under this title of "Natural History" there were included very heterogeneous constituents — that, for example, geology and mineralogy were, in many respects, widely different from botany and zoology; that a man might obtain an extensive knowledge of the structure and functions of plants and animals, without having need to enter upon the study of geology or mineralogy, and *vice versâ*; and, further as knowledge advanced, it became clear that there was a great analogy, a very close alliance, between those two sciences of botany and zoology which deal with living beings, while they are much more widely separated from all other studies. It is due to Buffon to remark that he clearly recognised this great fact. He says: "Ces deux genres d'êtres organisés [les animaux et les végétaux] ont beaucoup plus de propriétés communes que de différences réelles." Therefore, it is not wonderful that, at the beginning of the present century, in two different countries, and so far as I know, without any intercommunication, two famous men clearly conceived the notion of uniting the sciences which deal with living matter into one whole, and of dealing with them as one discipline. In fact, I may say there were three men to whom this idea occurred contemporaneously, although there were but two who carried it into effect, and only one who worked it out completely. The persons to whom I refer were the eminent physiologist Bichat, and the great naturalist Lamarck, in France; and a distinguished

German, Treviranus. Bichat[1] assumed the existence of a special group of "physiological" sciences. Lamarck, in a work published in 1801,[2] for the first time made use of the name "Biologie" from the two Greek words which signify a discourse upon life and living things. About the same time it occurred to Treviranus, that all those sciences which deal with living matter are essentially and fundamentally one, and ought to be treated as a whole; and, in the year 1802, he published the first volume of what he also called "Biologie." Treviranus's great merit lies in this, that he worked out his idea, and wrote the very remarkable book to which I refer. It consists of six volumes, and occupied its author for twenty years — from 1802 to 1822.

That is the origin of the term "Biology;" and that is how it has come about that all clear thinkers and lovers of consistent nomenclature have substituted for the old confusing name of "Natural History," which has conveyed so many meanings, the term "Biology" which denotes the whole of the sciences which deal with living things, whether they be animals or whether they be plants. Some little time ago — in the course of this year, I think — I was favoured by a learned classic, Dr. Field of Norwich, with a disquisition, in which he endeavoured to prove that, from a philological point of view, neither Treviranus nor Lamarck had any right to coin this new word "Biology" for their purpose; that, in fact, the Greek word "Bios" had relation only to human life and human affairs, and that a different word was employed by the Greeks when they wished to speak of the life of animals and plants. So Dr. Field tells us we are all wrong in using the term biology, and that we ought to employ another; only he is not quite sure about the propriety of that which he proposes as a substitute. It is a somewhat hard one — "zootocology." I am sorry we are wrong, because we are likely to continue so. In these matters we must have some sort of "Statute of Limitations." When a name has been employed for half-a-century, persons of authority[3] have been using it, and its sense has become well understood, I am afraid that people will go on using it, whatever the weight of philological objection.

Now that we have arrived at the origin of this word "Biology," the next point to consider is: What ground does it cover? I have said that, in its strict technical sense, it denotes all the phenomena which are exhibited by living things, as distinguished from those which are not living; but while that is all very well, so long as we confine ourselves to the lower animals and to plants, it lands us in considerable difficulties when we reach the higher forms of living things. For whatever view we may entertain about the nature of man, one thing is perfectly certain, that he is a living creature. Hence, if our definition is to be interpreted strictly, we must include man and all his ways and works under the head of Biology; in which case, we should find that psychology, politics, and political economy would be absorbed into the province of Biology. In fact, civil history would be merged in natural history. In strict logic it may be hard to object to this course, because no one can doubt that the rudiments and outlines of our own mental phenomena are traceable among the lower animals. They have their economy and their polity, and if, as is always admitted, the polity of bees and the commonwealth of wolves fall within the purview of the biologist proper, it becomes hard to say why we should not include therein human affairs, which in so many cases resemble those of the bees in zealous getting, and are not without a certain parity in the proceedings of the wolves. The real fact is that we biologists are a self-sacrificing people; and inasmuch as, on a moderate estimate, there are about a quarter of a million different species of animals and plants to know about already, we feel that we have more than sufficient territory. There has been a sort of practical convention by which we give up to a different branch of science what Bacon and Hobbes would have called "Civil History." That branch of science has constituted itself under the head of Sociology. I may use phraseology which, at present, will be well understood and say that we have allowed that province of Biology to become autonomous; but I should like you to recollect that that is a sacrifice, and that you should not be surprised if it occasionally happens that you see a biologist apparently trespassing in the region of philosophy or politics; or meddling with human education; because, after all, that is a part of his kingdom which he has only voluntarily forsaken.

Having now defined the meaning of the word Biology, and having indicated the general scope of Biological Science, I turn to my second question, which is — Why should we study Biology? Possibly the time may come when that will seem a very odd question. That we, living creatures, should not feel a certain amount of interest in what it is that constitutes our life will eventually, under altered ideas of the fittest objects of human inquiry, appear to be a singular phenomenon; but, at present, judging by the practice of teachers and educators, Biology would seem to be a topic that does not concern us at all. I propose to put before you a few considerations with which I dare say many will be familiar already, but which will suffice to show — not fully, because to demonstrate this point fully would take a great many lectures — that there are some very good and substantial reasons why it may be advisable that we should know something about this branch of human learning.

I myself entirely agree with another sentiment of the philosopher of Malmesbury, "that the scope of all speculation is the performance of some action or thing to be done," and I have not any very great respect for, or interest in, mere knowing as such. I judge of the value of human pursuits by their bearing upon human interests; in other words, by their utility; but I should like that we should quite clearly understand what it is that we mean by this word "utility." In an Englishman's mouth it generally means that by which we get pudding or praise, or both. I have no doubt that is one meaning of the word utility, but it by no means includes all I mean by utility. I think that knowledge of every kind is useful in proportion as it tends to give people right ideas, which are essential to the foundation of right practice, and to remove wrong ideas, which are the no less essential foundations and fertile mothers of every description of error in practice. And inasmuch as, whatever practical people may say, this world is, after all, absolutely governed by ideas, and very often by the wildest and most hypothetical ideas, it is a matter of the very greatest importance that our theories of things, and even of things that seem a long way apart from our daily lives, should be as far as possible true, and as far as possible removed from error. It is not only in the coarser practical sense of the word "utility," but in this higher and broader sense, that I measure the value of the study of biology by its utility; and I shall try to point out to you that you will feel the need of some knowledge of biology at a great many turns of this present nineteenth century life of ours. For example, most of us attach great importance to the conception which we entertain of the position of man in this universe and his relation to the rest of nature. We have almost all been told, and most of us hold by the tradition, that man occupies an isolated and peculiar position in nature; that though he is in the world he is not of the world; that his relations to things about him are of a remote character; that his origin is recent, his duration likely to be short, and that he is the great central figure round which other things in this world revolve. But this is not what the biologist tells us.

At the present moment you will be kind enough to separate me from them, because it is in no way essential to my present argument that I should advocate their views. Don't suppose that I am saying this for the purpose of escaping the responsibility of their beliefs; indeed, at other times and in other places, I do not think that point has been left doubtful; but I want clearly to point out to you that for my present argument they may all be wrong; and, nevertheless, my argument will hold good. The biologists tell us that all this is an entire mistake. They turn to the physical organisation of man. They examine his whole structure, his bony frame and all that clothes it. They resolve him into the finest particles into which the microscope will enable them to break him up. They consider the performance of his various functions and activities, and they look at the manner in which he occurs on the surface of the world. Then they turn to other animals, and taking the first handy domestic animal — say a dog — they profess to be able to demonstrate that the analysis of the dog leads them, in gross, to precisely the same results as the analysis of the man; that they find almost identically the same bones, having the same relations; that they can name the muscles of the dog by the names of the muscles of the man, and the nerves of the dog by those of the nerves of the man, and that, such structures and organs of sense as we find in the man such also we find in the dog; they analyse the brain and spinal cord, and they find that the nomenclature which fits the one answers for the other. They carry their microscopic inquiries in the case of the dog as far as they can, and they find that his body is resolvable into the same elements as those of the man. Moreover, they trace back the dog's and the man's development, and they find that, at a certain stage of their existence, the two creatures are not distinguishable the one from the other; they find that the dog and his kind have a certain distribution over the surface of the world, comparable in its way to the distribution of the human species. What is true of the dog they tell us is true of all the higher animals; and they assert that they can lay down a common plan for the whole of these creatures, and regard the man and the dog, the horse and the ox as minor modifications of one great fundamental unity. Moreover, the investigations of the last three-quarters of a century have proved, they tell us, that similar inquiries, carried out through all the different kinds of animals which are met with in nature, will lead us, not in one straight series, but by many roads, step by step, gradation by gradation, from man, at the summit, to specks of animated jelly at the bottom of the series. So that the idea of Leibnitz, and of Bonnet, that animals form a great scale of being, in which there are a series of gradations from the most complicated form to the lowest and simplest; that idea, though not exactly in the form in which it was propounded by those philosophers, turns out to be substantially correct. More than this, when biologists pursue their investigations into the vegetable world, they find that they can, in the same way, follow out the structure of the plant, from the most gigantic and complicated trees down through a similar series of gradations, until they arrive at specks of animated jelly, which they are puzzled to distinguish from those specks which they reached by the animal road.

Thus, biologists have arrived at the conclusion that a fundamental uniformity of structure pervades the animal and vegetable worlds, and that plants and animals differ from one another simply as diverse modifications of the same great general plan.

Again, they tell us the same story in regard to the study of function. They admit the large and important interval which, at the present time, separates the manifestations of the mental faculties observable in the higher forms of mankind, and even in the lower forms, such as we know them, from those exhibited by other animals; but, at the same time, they tell us that the foundations, or rudiments, of almost all the faculties of man are to be met with in the lower animals; that there is a unity of mental faculty as well as of bodily structure, and that, here also, the difference is a difference of degree and not of kind. I said "almost all," for a reason. Among the many distinctions which have been drawn between the lower creatures and ourselves, there is one which is hardly ever insisted on,[4] but which may be very fitly spoken of in a place so largely devoted to Art as that in which we are assembled. It is this, that while, among various kinds of animals, it is possible to discover traces of all the other faculties of man, especially the faculty of mimicry, yet that particular form of mimicry which shows itself in the imitation of form, either by modelling or by drawing, is not to be met with. As far as I know, there is no sculpture or modelling, and decidedly no painting or drawing, of animal origin, I mention the fact, in order that such comfort may be derived therefrom as artists may feel inclined to take.

If what the biologists tell us is true, it will be needful to get rid of our erroneous conceptions of man, and of his place in nature, and to substitute right ones for them. But it is impossible to form any judgment as to whether the biologists are right or wrong, unless we are able to appreciate the nature of the arguments which they have to offer.

One would almost think this to be a self-evident proposition. I wonder what a scholar would say to the man who should undertake to criticise a difficult passage in a Greek play, but who obviously had not acquainted himself with the rudiments of Greek grammar. And yet, before giving positive opinions about these high questions of Biology, people not only do not seem to think it necessary to be acquainted with the grammar of the subject, but they have not even mastered the alphabet. You find criticism and denunciation showered about by persons, who, not only have not attempted to go through the discipline necessary to enable them to be judges, but who have not even reached that stage of emergence from ignorance in which the knowledge that such a discipline is necessary dawns upon the mind. I have had to watch with some attention — in fact I have been favoured with a good deal of it myself — the sort of criticism with which biologists and biological teachings are visited. I am told every now and then that there is a "brilliant article"[5] in so-and-so, in which we are all demolished. I used to read these things once, but I am getting old now, and I have ceased to attend very much to this cry of "wolf." When one does read any of these productions, what one finds generally, on the face of it, is that the brilliant critic is devoid of even the elements of biological knowledge, and that his brilliancy is like the light given out by the crackling of thorns under a pot of which Solomon speaks. So far as I recollect, Solomon makes use of the image for purposes of comparison; but I will not proceed further into that matter.

Two things must be obvious: in the first place, that every man who has the interests of truth at heart must earnestly desire that every well-founded and just criticism that can be made should be made; but that, in the second place, it is essential to anybody's being able to benefit by criticism, that the critic should know what he is talking about, and be in a position to form a mental image of the facts symbolised by the words he uses. If not, it is as obvious in the case of a biological argument, as it is in that of a historical or philological discussion, that such criticism is a mere waste of time on the part of its author, and wholly undeserving of attention on the part of those who are criticised. Take it then as an illustration of the importance of biological study, that thereby alone are men able to form something like a rational conception of what constitutes valuable criticism of the teachings of biologists.[6]

Next, I may mention another bearing of biological knowledge—a more practical one in the ordinary sense of the word. Consider the theory of infectious disease. Surely that is of interest to all of us. Now the theory of infectious disease is rapidly being elucidated by biological study. It is possible to produce, from among the lower animals, examples of devastating diseases which spread in the same manner as our infectious disorders, and which are certainly and unmistakably caused by living organisms. This fact renders it possible, at any rate, that that doctrine of the causation of infectious disease which is known under the name of "the germ theory" may be well-founded; and, if so, it must needs lead to the most important practical measures in dealing with those terrible visitations. It may be well that the general, as well as the professional, public should have a sufficient knowledge of biological truths to be able to take a rational interest in the discussion of such problems, and to see, what I think they may hope to see, that, to those who possess a sufficient elementary knowledge of Biology, they are not all quite open questions.

Let me mention another important practical illustration of the value of biological study. Within the last forty years the theory of agriculture has been revolutionised. The researches of Liebig, and those of our own Lawes and Gilbert, have had a bearing upon that branch of industry the importance of which cannot be overestimated; but the whole of these new views have grown out of the better explanation of certain processes which go on in plants; and which, of course, form a part of the subject-matter of Biology.

I might go on multiplying these examples, but I see that the clock won't wait for me, and I must therefore pass to the third question to which

I referred: Granted that Biology is something worth studying, what is the best way of studying it? Here I must point out that, since Biology is a physical science, the method of studying it must needs be analogous to that which is followed in the other physical sciences. It has now long been recognised that, if a man wishes to be a chemist, it is not only necessary that he should read chemical books and attend chemical lectures, but that he should actually perform the fundamental experiments in the laboratory for himself, and thus learn exactly what the words which he finds in his books and hears from his teachers, mean. If he does not do so, he may read till the crack of doom, but he will never know much about chemistry. That is what every chemist will tell you, and the physicist will do the same for his branch of science. The great changes and improvements in physical and chemical scientific education, which have taken place of late, have all resulted from the combination of practical teaching with the reading of books and with the hearing of lectures. The same thing is true in Biology. Nobody will ever know anything about Biology except in a dilettante "paper-philosopher" way, who contents himself with reading books on botany, zoology, and the like; and the reason of this is simple and easy to understand. It is that all language is merely symbolical of the things of which it treats; the more complicated the things, the more bare is the symbol, and the more its verbal definition requires to be supplemented by the information derived directly from the handling, and the seeing, and the touching of the thing symbolised: — that is really what is at the bottom of the whole matter. It is plain common sense, as all truth, in the long run, is only common sense clarified. If you want a man to be a tea merchant, you don't tell him to read books about China or about tea, but you put him into a tea-merchant's office where he has the handling, the smelling, and the tasting of tea. Without the sort of knowledge which can be gained only in this practical way, his exploits as a tea merchant will soon come to a bankrupt termination. The "paper-philosophers" are under the delusion that physical science can be mastered as literary accomplishments are acquired, but unfortunately it is not so. You may read any quantity of books, and you may be almost as ignorant as you were at starting, if you don't have, at the back of your minds, the change for words in definite images which can only be acquired through the operation of your observing faculties on the phenomena of nature.

It may be said: — "That is all very well, but you told us just now that there are probably something like a quarter of a million different kinds of living and extinct animals and plants, and a human life could not suffice for the examination of one-fiftieth part of all these." That is true, but then comes the great convenience of the way things are arranged; which is, that although there are these immense numbers of different kinds of living things in existence, yet they are built up, after all, upon marvellously few plans.

There are certainly more than 100,000 species of insects, and yet anybody who knows one insect — if a properly chosen one — will be able to have a very fair conception of the structure of the whole. I do not mean to say he will know that structure thoroughly, or as well as it is desirable he should know it; but he will have enough real knowledge to enable him to understand what he reads, to have genuine images in his mind of those structures which become so variously modified in all the forms of insects he has not seen. In fact, there are such things as types of form among animals and vegetables, and for the purpose of getting a definite knowledge of what constitutes the leading modifications of animal and plant life, it is not needful to examine more than a comparatively small number of animals and plants.

Let me tell you what we do in the biological laboratory which is lodged in a building adjacent to this. There I lecture to a class of students daily for about four-and-a-half months, and my class have, of course, their text-books; but the essential part of the whole teaching, and that which I regard as really the most important part of it, is a laboratory for practical work, which is simply a room with all the appliances needed for ordinary dissection. We have tables properly arranged in regard to light, microscopes, and dissecting instruments, and we work through the structure of a certain number of animals and plants. As, for example, among the plants, we take a yeast plant, a *Protococcus*, a common mould, a *Chara*, a fern, and some flowering plant; among animals we examine such things as an *Amœba*, a *Vorticella*, and a fresh-water polype. We dissect a star-fish, an earth-worm, a snail, a squid, and a fresh-water mussel. We examine a lobster and a cray-fish, and a black beetle. We go on to a common skate, a cod-fish, a frog, a tortoise, a pigeon, and a rabbit, and that takes us about all the time we have to give. The purpose of this course is not to make skilled dissectors, but to give every student a clear and definite conception, by means of sense-images, of the characteristic structure of each of the leading modifications of the animal kingdom; and that is perfectly possible, by going no further than the length of that list of forms which I have enumerated. If a man knows the structure of the animals I have mentioned, he has a clear and exact, however limited, apprehension of the essential features of the organisation of all those great divisions of the animal and vegetable kingdoms to which the forms I have mentioned severally belong. And it then becomes possible for him to read with profit; because every time he meets with the name of a structure, he has a definite image in his mind of what the name means in the particular creature he is reading about, and therefore the reading is not mere reading. It is not mere repetition of words; but every term employed in the description, we will say, of a horse, or of an elephant, will call up the image of the things he had seen in the rabbit, and he is able to form a distinct conception of that which he has not seen, as a modification of that which he has seen.

I find this system to yield excellent results; and I have no hesitation whatever in saying, that any one who has gone through such a course, attentively, is in a better position to form a conception of the great truths of Biology, especially of morphology (which is what we chiefly deal with), than if he had merely read all the books on that topic put together.

The connection of this discourse with the Loan Collection of Scientific Apparatus arises out of the exhibition in that collection of certain aids to our laboratory work. Such of you as have visited that very interesting collection may have noticed a series of diagrams and of preparations illustrating the structure of a frog. Those diagrams and preparations have been made for the use of the students in the biological laboratory. Similar diagrams and preparations illustrating the structure of all the other forms of life we examine, are either made or in course of preparation. Thus the student has before him, first, a picture of the structure he ought to see; secondly, the structure itself worked out; and if with these aids, and such needful explanations and practical hints as a demonstrator can supply, he cannot make out the facts for himself in the materials supplied to him, he had better take to some other pursuit than that of biological science.

I should have been glad to have said a few words about the use of museums in the study of Biology, but I see that my time is becoming short, and I have yet another question to answer. Nevertheless I must, at the risk of wearying you, say a word or two upon the important subject of museums. Without doubt there are no helps to the study of Biology, or rather to some branches of it, which are, or may be, more important than natural history museums; but, in order to take this place in regard to Biology, they must be museums of the future. The museums of the present do not, by any means, do so much for us as they might do. I do not wish to particularise, but I dare say many of you, seeking knowledge, or in the laudable desire to employ a holiday usefully, have visited some great natural history museum. You have walked through a quarter of a mile of animals, more or less well stuffed, with their long names written out underneath them; and, unless your experience is very different from that of most people, the upshot of it all is that you leave that splendid pile with sore feet, a bad headache, and a general idea that the animal kingdom is a "mighty maze without a plan." I do not think that a museum which brings about this result does all that may be reasonably expected from such an institution. What is needed in a collection of natural history is that it should be made as accessible and as useful as possible, on the one hand to the general public, and on the other to scientific workers. That need is not met by constructing a sort of happy hunting-ground of miles of glass cases; and, under the pretence of exhibiting everything, putting the maximum amount of obstacle in the way of those who wish properly to see anything.

What the public want is easy and unhindered access to such a collection as they can understand and appreciate; and what the men of science want is similar access to the materials of science. To this end the vast mass of objects of natural history should be divided into two parts — one open to the public, the other to men of science, every day. The former division should exemplify all the more important and interesting forms of life. Explanatory tablets should be attached to them, and catalogues containing clearly-written popular expositions of the general significance of the objects exhibited should be provided. The latter should contain, packed into a comparatively small space, in rooms adapted for working purposes, the objects of purely scientific interest. For example, we will say I am an ornithologist. I go to examine a collection of birds. It is a positive nuisance to have them stuffed. It is not only sheer waste, but I have to reckon with the ideas of the bird-stuffer, while, if I have the skin and nobody has interfered with it, I can form my own judgment as to what the bird was like. For ornithological purposes, what is needed is not glass cases full of stuffed birds on perches, but convenient drawers into each of which a great quantity of skins will go. They occupy no great space and do not require any expenditure beyond their original cost. But for the edification of the public, who want to learn indeed, but do not seek for minute and technical knowledge, the case is different. What one of the general public walking into a collection of birds desires to see is not all the birds that can be got together. He does not want to compare a hundred species of the sparrow tribe side by side; but he wishes to know what a bird is, and what are the great modifications of bird structure, and to be able to get at that knowledge easily. What will best serve his purpose is a comparatively small number of birds carefully selected, and artistically, as well as accurately, set up; with their different ages, their nests, their young, their eggs, and their skeletons side by side; and in accordance with the admirable plan which is pursued in this museum, a tablet, telling the spectator in legible characters what they are and what they mean. For the instruction and recreation of the public such a typical collection would be of far greater value than any many-acred imitation of Noah's ark.

Lastly comes the question as to when biological study may best be pursued. I do not see any valid reason why it should not be made, to a certain extent, a part of ordinary school training. I have long advocated this view, and I am perfectly certain that it can be carried out with ease, and not only with ease, but with very considerable profit to those who are taught; but then such instruction must be adapted to the minds and needs of the scholars. They used to have a very odd way of teaching the classical languages when I was a boy. The first task set you was to learn the rules of the Latin grammar in the Latin language — that being the language you were going to learn! I thought then that this was an odd way of learning a language, but did not venture to rebel against the judgment of my superiors. Now, perhaps, I am not so modest as I was then, and I allow myself to think that it was a very absurd fashion. But it would be no less absurd, if we were to set about teaching Biology by putting into the hands of boys a series of definitions of the classes and orders of the animal kingdom, and making them repeat them by heart. That is so very favourite a method of teaching, that I sometimes fancy the spirit of the old classical system has entered into the new scientific system, in which case I would much rather that any pretence at scientific teaching were abolished altogether. What really has to be done is to get into the young mind some notion of what animal and vegetable life is. In this matter, you have to consider practical convenience as well as other things. There are difficulties in the way of a lot of boys making messes with slugs and snails; it might not work in practice. But there is a very convenient and handy animal which everybody has at hand, and that is himself; and it is a very easy and simple matter to obtain common plants. Hence the general truths of anatomy and physiology can be taught to young people in a very real fashion by dealing with the broad facts of human structure. Such viscera as they cannot very well examine in themselves, such as hearts, lungs, and livers, may be obtained from the nearest butcher's shop. In respect to teaching something about the biology of plants, there is no practical difficulty, because almost any of the common plants will do, and plants do not make a mess—at least they do not make an unpleasant mess; so that, in my judgment, the best form of Biology for teaching to very young people is elementary human physiology on the one hand, and the elements of botany on the other; beyond that I do not think it will be feasible to advance for some time to come. But then I see no reason why, in secondary schools, and in the Science Classes which are under the control of the Science and Art Department—and which I may say, in passing, have, in my judgment, done so very much for the diffusion of a knowledge of science over the country—we should not hope to see instruction in the elements of Biology carried out, not perhaps to the same extent, but still upon somewhat the same principle as here. There is no difficulty, when you have to deal with students of the ages of 15 or 16, in practising a little dissection and in getting a notion of, at any rate, the four or five great modifications of the animal form; and the like is true in regard to the higher anatomy of plants.

While, lastly, to all those who are studying biological science with a view to their own edification merely, or with the intention of becoming zoologists or botanists; to all those who intend to pursue physiology— and especially to those who propose to employ the working years of their lives in the practice of medicine—I say that there is no training so fitted, or which may be of such important service to them, as the discipline in practical biological work which I have sketched out as being pursued in the laboratory hard by.

I may add that, beyond all these different classes of persons who may profit by the study of Biology, there is yet one other. I remember, a number of years ago, that a gentleman who was a vehement opponent of Mr. Darwin's views and had written some terrible articles against them, applied to me to know what was the best way in which he could acquaint himself with the strongest arguments in favour of evolution. I wrote back, in all good faith and simplicity, recommending him to go through a course of comparative anatomy and physiology, and then to study development. I am sorry to say he was very much displeased, as people often are with good advice. Notwithstanding this discouraging result, I venture, as a parting word, to repeat the suggestion, and to say to all the more or less acute lay and clerical "paper-philosophers"[7] who venture into the regions of biological controversy — Get a little sound, thorough, practical, elementary instruction in biology.

[1]   See the distinction between the "sciences physiques" and the "sciences physiologiques" in the "Anatomic Générale," 1801.

[2]   "Hydrogeologie," an. x. (1801).

[3]   "The term *Biology*, which means exactly what we wish to express, *the Science of Life*, has often been used, and has of late become not uncommon, among good writers." — Whewell, "Philosophy of the Inductive Sciences," vol. i. p. 544 (edition of 1847).

[4]   I think that my friend Professor Allman was the first to draw attention to it.

[5]   Galileo was troubled by a sort of people whom he called "paper philosophers," because they fancied that the true reading of nature was to be detected by the collation of texts. The race is not extinct, but, as of old, brings forth its "winds of doctrine" by which the weathercock heads among us are much exercised.

[6]   Some critics do not even take the trouble to read. I have recently been adjured with much solemnity, to state publicly why I have "changed my opinion" as to the value of the palæontological evidence of the occurrence of evolution.

To this my reply is, Why should I, when that statement was made seven years ago? An address delivered from the Presidential Chair of the Geological Society, in 1870, may be said to be a public document, inasmuch as it not only appeared in the *Journal* of that learned body, but was re-published, in 1873, in a volume of "Critiques and Addresses," to which my name is attached. Therein will be found a pretty full statement of my reasons for enunciating two propositions: (1) that "when we turn to the higher *Vertebrata*, the results of recent investigations, however we may sift and criticise them, seem to me to leave a clear balance in favour of the evolution of living forms one from another;" and (2) that the case of the horse is one which "will stand rigorous criticism."

Thus I do not see clearly in what way I can be said to have changed my opinion, except in the way of intensifying it, when in consequence of the accumulation of similar evidence since 1870, I recently spoke of the denial of evolution as not worth serious consideration.

[7]   Writers of this stamp are fond of talking about the Baconian method. I beg them therefore to lay to heart these two weighty sayings of the herald of Modern Science: —

"Syllogismus ex propositionibus constat, propositiones ex verbis, verba notionum tesseræ sunt. Itaque si notiones ipsæ (*id quod basis rei est*) confusæ sint et temere a rebus abstractæ, nihil in iis quæ superstruuntur est firmitudinis." — "Novum Organon," ii. 14.

"Huic autem vanitati nonnulli ex modernis summa levitate ita indulserunt, ut in primo capitulo Geneseos et in libro Job et aliis scripturis sacris, philosophiam naturalem fundare conati sint; *inter vivos quærentes mortua*." — *Ibid.*, 65.